Here's What I Need You to Know

You to Know

Shari Franklin

ISBN: 978-1-957723-32-7 Hard Cover
       978-1-957723-33-4 Soft Cover

Franklin. Shari.

Edited by: Amy Ashby

Published by Warren Publishing
Charlotte, NC
www.warrenpublishing.net
Printed in the United States

This book is dedicated to women everywhere.
May we find commonality in our struggles,
strength in our similarities, and the guts to never
live in shame or fear of our truth.

Table of Contents

HERE'S WHAT I NEED YOU TO KNOW
{about this book}

"Y ou should write a book."
        I have had that sentence uttered at me and typed to me. It
        has come via social media posts and text messages, voice mail,
and email. And it has even been relayed on occasion during an actual
phone call.

I have avoided it for who knows how many reasons.

What would I write about?

Self-help, survival, memoir, how-to, what-not-to-do ... the
categories are endless.

Who would read it? And what could I offer that is not out
there already?

Everything is available at our fingertips. Advice, photos, gossip,
recipes, lyrics, an old high school boyfriend's current photographs ...
If we want to see it or read it or know about it, we can. Instantly.

I have always had one rule for my writing: **I only write when I
know it is time to write.**

Something must inspire me.

Something must tug at my core and urge the words forth.

Something deep inside must pulse, and it must become almost
uncontainable.

Then ... that is when I write.

I also only write about what I know.

My list of qualifications is one sentence long: I was a teacher, and now I am a mom.

What I know is limited.

What I know is: motherhood and grace and hurt and healing. Fortitude and acceptance and love and forgiveness.

This is not the Bible. It is not Bible study. It is not meant to replace the word of God, sage advice, Grandma's wisdom, or common sense. My experiences have taken the words that make up my humanity and have woven together a beautiful life. All of that has led to this.

I may not know a lot of things, but here's what I need you to know: Every story might not be for you. But every story is for someone.

May the words written here inspire you to live a life of action, acceptance, love, and healing.

HERE'S WHAT I NEED YOU TO KNOW
{about vacations}

I absolutely love a vacation.

Actually, based on what I have learned via the internet, I love a "trip." Apparently, if one does *any* laundry, cooks *any* meal, or plans *any* event during a family getaway, the online gods deem it a "trip" and not a "vacation." I have therefore determined that I have, in fact, *never* actually been on a vacation.

Regardless, any time my family packs up what feels like most of our belongings, gases up the car (or cars, now that everyone is older, and we have more people. So. Many. People.), and heads out to someplace with an address different than where we receive our bills, we call it a "vacation."

Traveling with family is always taking a chance. There is the ever-present risk that overexposure to one another will result in serious burns. There is not enough aloe on the planet for that kind of sting. And since there is no preventative spray to coat our families with, the best protection is to limit the list of those invited to the kids we have raised and their significant others. The farther out on the branches of the family tree the invitations extend, the greater the possibility for all the branches to just break right off and land in a huge heap on the ground. At that point, you might as well just pour some gasoline on it, set it all on fire, grab a chair, and wait for the fireworks.

Thus far, keeping the guest list small has limited our casualties.

The worst part of a vacation, though, *has* to be the ending, which always feels like it starts about half a day too early. You know how it goes: When the vacation starts, you count time by how many days you have been there. "It's only been one day? It feels like we have already been here *forever!*"

Then, on a day out of nowhere that feels way too soon, you realize you are now counting time in days *left*. The math never seems to add up. Vacation math is a scam. You cannot convince me otherwise. I have never been on a vacation where I came home saying, "That was just a little too long."

Is it only me? Please tell me it's not! Not only does the countdown begin prematurely, but so does preparing to vacate the vacation. The exit strategy usually begins the day before checkout, with someone (Mom) making mental checklists and a time line. It's why you don't sleep well the last night of vacation: Someone (Mom) has to stay up late and wash the wet bathing suits from the after-dark swim. Someone (Mom) has to clean up the kitchen and make sure the trash is all bagged up ...

You never get to sleep in on the last day of vacation either. It always means rising early to pick up and pack up and load up. Whether you drove, flew, took a boat, or used some combination of these, the decampment process is relatively the same. It is the point at which I always ask myself the following two questions: Did we bring *all* these things with us, and *who* allowed the kids to pack all this stuff? So. Much. Stuff?

I mean, honestly ... did every girl need her *own* curling iron and hair dryer and pillow? Don't we stay at decent places so we can come without our own pillows? And did each guy *have* to bring four hats, three fishing rods, and all the underwear they own?

We try to stay in places with a washer and dryer for the sole purpose of being able to pack less. Clearly, that's only the expectation. Maybe that is just *my* expectation. I may need to work on my communication skills ... The reality is, my family packs like everyone went back in while the house was on fire and grabbed everything they could hold.

This makes for a lengthy, day-of double-checking process. You know, when the bathrooms have to be double-checked by someone

(Mom) to be sure nothing was left behind. Also the back porch. And the balcony. And the deck. Moms all across the universe did a huge victory dance when hotels finally started putting bed frames *directly on the floor* so mamas had one less place to search for the random item from home that would shatter the earth if forgotten.

Then, there is all the stuff we possess now as a result of "vacation brain." Someone in our group now owns a three-foot-tall Minion stuffed animal, won after twenty-four dollars worth of driveway-quality basketball at a theme-park price. We have more plastic, free-refill cups with straws than we ever could possibly need. We paid for them, so you best believe we got them.

All of them.

Did we ever actually get a refill? Probably not.

Did we still get all the cups? Absolutely.

When we are loaded down with various leftover food and beverages and sunscreen and electronics, each one of us with our sun-kissed skin processes our goodbye in our own way. (If my kids ever stop saying, "Byyyyyyyeeeee pool … Byyyyyyyeeeee hot tub" as they stand on the balcony one last time, I'd surely be disappointed.)

Here's what I need you to know:

No matter how many last-day early alarms have to be set, it's worth it. The moments we share with the people we love make all the preparation valid. Sometimes, on that dreaded last night of vacation, I like to watch my people sleep. I love to know that we have played hard, created lifelong memories, and strengthened the bonds we already share. No matter what it took to get there, my heart is always fuller knowing we somehow made it happen.

Vacation planning means sacrifice. It may mean fewer meals out and more meals at home. It might mean fewer convenience-store trips and fewer date nights and fewer splurge purchases. For many, it may even require setting aside some home-improvement plans and delaying the purchase of things that now are more "wants" rather than "needs."

Vacations do not generally just "happen" to people. You have to make a vacation happen. You work hard and rearrange schedules, and the larger the family, the further out it seems the planning has to start.

If you haven't worked hard, set aside, saved up, and planned ahead, you will head home after all is said and done in debt and extremely disappointed. **The flip side is also true:** if you overplan, overschedule, set your expectations unrealistically high, or put pressure on everyone to have fun in the way YOU decide is appropriate, you'll leave just as let down.

Vacation is the perfect time to pay too much for a burger, justify washing six items as an entire load of laundry, leave clothes out of suitcases, hang nothing up, stay up too late, forget about eating healthy foods, and do things out of the ordinary.

It should feel like home in the sense that you're surrounded by loved ones, but it also should feel different enough to tempt us to splurge and be spontaneous and fall into bed at night reminiscing over the events of the day, exhausted with anticipation for what's to come.

Make vacations happen! Whether it is a weeklong trip far away or a weekend closer to home—plan it. If it means searching for deals and borrowing necessities and getting out of your comfort zone—just do it.

We are always better after a break from the normal. Our eyes are more open, our minds think more clearly, and our families feel a little tighter. Whatever it takes, make it happen.

It will always be a worthwhile investment.

HERE'S WHAT I NEED YOU TO KNOW
{about scars}

I was at the pool recently. More specifically, I was floating around in the lazy river, minding my own business. There are some advantages to having older children. Being left alone in the lazy river is one of them.

I noticed this lady in front of me, who was stunning. She was floating along with a man, who I presumed was her husband. She was of Latin descent, with impossibly perfect tan skin, beautiful long hair, gorgeous eyes ... She was just captivating.

We were obviously not the same age. I'm sure I had ten, maybe even fifteen, years on her, but I still found myself wishing that I looked like her, wondering why I didn't have that tone to my pasty white skin or that overall "passersby do a double take" kind of look. She looked like a magazine cover; I felt like the back page. At some point during our journey, she turned toward the front, away from me. It was at that moment that I noticed the scars on her back.

I cannot possibly imagine what would've created scars like that. It literally looked like she had placed her back on a hot grill. The wounds were healed completely, but it was obvious that something traumatic had happened to cause them. She had been through *something*. She had dealt with some sort of incident that left its mark ... literally.

I remember immediately thinking to myself, *I guess I don't want to be like her after all.*

I'm not proud that I thought that. I'm just telling you that's what I thought. All of a sudden, my perspective had shifted when I could see the entire picture.

Here's what I need you to know:
Maybe if we could truly see people, scars and all, it would make us less likely to covet someone else's life.

Maybe in our social media-filled, filtered world, we spend all our time seeing only what people want us to see. We spend so much time looking at what we think people have, how we think they live, how much better we think they have it than we do, that we can't truly see what it has cost some people to get to where they are.

Maybe if we could see the price tags of their journeys, we would find more contentment in our own accounts. Maybe knowing the cost others had paid for the life they were living would change our perspective on our own journeys. We would be happy with the hands we have been dealt, regardless of the faces on the cards.

Everyone has scars.

Sometimes they are on the outside, and they are visible. Sometimes they look like bruises and markings. Sometimes they are front and center for all to see.

But sometimes, they are deep on the inside, hidden away from view. Sometimes they look like adultery and verbal abuse and mental health issues.

Maybe our world could be a very different place if we all stopped looking across the fence into the neighbor's yard.

Maybe what we see is what we have decided to see or what we have been conditioned to see.

Maybe we have all become accustomed to hiding our scars.

We would be wise to be very careful when we look at someone's life and find ourselves wishing it were us.

We don't know the cost someone paid to have that life.

HERE'S WHAT I NEED YOU TO KNOW
{about old things}

I found an old box spring the other day. It had been tucked away in "my side" of the storage building beside our house. That's the name I gave to the side I wanted the husband to keep his stuff out of. You know, that space that *could* remain clutter free and mess free if he (and the kids) would just stay out!

This box spring served our family well. At one time or another, it provided support for all seven people living here. It was a constant structure through the rough adolescent years and the ever-tiring tween and teen years.

It did not cost a lot. Nothing we own ever does. It was very basic; it did not need any special attention to do the job it was designed to do. It was right there as the seemingly invisible stepsister of the mattress, basically doing all the hard work and heavy lifting, yet unseen and unnoted. *Always a bridesmaid, never a bride.*

This particular box spring also kept many guests from making their place of rest on the floor. It struggled under the weight of the heavier years. It rested during the leaner times. Its cover was marred by lack of attention and overuse. Neglected, it was shoved away, out of sight. It seemed like the time had come … Perhaps its job was done.

So today, I almost handed it over to the trash heap. I felt like the time for it to be a necessary part of the picture was over. And then, right there between storage and trash, right when it seemed destined for the landfill, I remembered what I had saved it for. I started tearing away at the covering. I cut and ripped. I pulled and clipped away. The actions required effort and struggle and pressure and intense frustration at times. But I *knew* what was underneath. When I was finished taking apart the box spring, a beautiful, metallic framework remained, ready for new life. Its potential was endless.

Here's what I need you to know:

Some of us have been tucked away for a while now. We have served our families well. We have provided support for any number of people and been a constant structure through the rough adolescent years and the ever-tiring tween and teen years. *Often, life looked like screaming matches and slamming doors and late-night tears.*

We have not cost a lot; our needs are very basic. *It looked like leftovers and boxed hair dye and pink-and-green drugstore mascara.*

We have not needed any special attention in order for us to do the job we were designed to do. *It looked like early mornings and missed meals and undercelebrated special days.*

We have been needed, but work unseen. *It looked like stocked fridges and made beds and clean floors.*

We have kept many people from making their place of rest on the floor. *It looked like slumber parties and friends on couches and whispered conversations.*

We have struggled under the weight of our heavier years. We have rested during the leaner times. *It looked like dieting and cutting carbs and trying to make house cleaning into actual exercise.*

We have had our covers marred by lack of attention and overuse. *It looked like stretch marks and late nights and lack of sleep.*

We have been shoved away, out of sight, when we were not needed. Perhaps the time had come, and our job was done. *It looked like graduations and college dorms and disappearing taillights.*

And now, right in the middle of the beginning of the end, we feel discarded and useless like we have been handed over to the trash heap.

We have felt like the time for us to be a necessary part of the picture is over.

Here's what I need you to know: **Your time is not over; your purpose is not fulfilled.**

Your number has not been called, and your contributions to this world are not over.

You are not washed up, used up, finished up, or laid up.

You are not done, over, ended, or unnecessary.

We find out what we have been saved for right when our purpose seems to have been fulfilled. Sometimes, we have to be cut and ripped. Sometimes, we have to be pulled apart and clipped away. Doing so will require effort and struggle and pressure and intense frustration at times—but what is underneath is beautiful. What is underneath will serve a whole different purpose in the coming years.

Step into tomorrow boldly and without reservation. You are ready for a new life. Your potential is endless.

Do not allow yourself to be intimidated by what possibilities are still out there.

Chase all your big dreams and follow your heart.

Do all the things that have scared you and have been put on hold while the little people have needed you.

This is your unveiling.

Your rebirth.

Your new season.

Embrace it!

HERE'S WHAT I NEED YOU TO KNOW
{about children}

Several months ago, I spent time in Florida—two glorious weeks, if anyone really cares or needs to know. The twins were supposed to have a national volleyball tournament scattered between those two weeks. And since the dates kept being tossed up and down, we just went ahead and booked a place for the full two weeks. We booked months early and paid in advance, so there was no way I was missing the opportunity. Two weeks of sunshine and no schedule and limited forced cooking? Sign me up, please.

I spent most of that time in the pool on a mermaid float that I purchased at Walmart for $4.79. I'm nothing if not fancy, after all. Since the girls are older, they were very capable of hanging out by the pool without me staring at them with a watchful eye 24/7. What that meant for me was, I had a lot of time to make that float a second home of sorts. It became like an extra appendage, mermaid tail and all. I would situate myself so as to not capsize, place my sunglasses *just right*, and try my best to drift off into an abyss of thoughtlessness. Call me a bad parent ... I've been called worse.

Without fail, each and every day, small children would arrive at the pool. Usually this would happen right after I had not so delicately boarded the float. They never needed to warm up to the water like I did. They just appeared virtually out of nowhere and plummeted directly into the water. They would yell and giggle and throw toys. And splash. *A lot.*

Without fail, every parent with those children spent their time saying the same phrase over and over again. They used different tones. They used different volumes. They used slightly different words, but the message was the same: Don't splash. And, in particular, I knew that they meant "don't splash the lady resting quietly on the float in the pool."

I remember those days well. I would see someone who was obviously in a different stage of life than myself taking advantage of some quiet time and simultaneously having that quiet time ruined by my five wild ones splashing around. It was stressful *for me* to try to keep them from bothering anyone, and it was stressful *for the kids* as well. They just wanted to relax and be, well, kids.

Here's what I need you to know:
Let the children splash!

Teach them to be respectful of those around them, but let's talk about the facts: Pools are for swimming in. Water splashes. People get wet.

It's an effort in futility for you to keep trying to prevent splashing, and it's an effort in futility for your children as well. I know you think the perfect scenario would be for you to watch your little ones quietly and politely swim around the pool like little angels without disturbing anyone. I wanted that as well. As a seasoned parent now, I can assure you—kids simply aren't designed that way.

And I, as the adult floating quietly in the pool, need to be mindful of that. If I don't want to get wet, I can move. If I don't want to be splashed, I can find any number of places to sit away from the water. And one of the things I enjoy most, when that chaos erupts, is to look that mama square in the eyes and give her permission to let her children splash. It's freeing for both of us.

Life is short.

The world is in utter chaos at times.

The future is so uncertain, and we are not promised another breath.

Let the littles be little. Let them splash.

HERE'S WHAT I NEED YOU TO KNOW
{about stages}

I have been a mama in stages.

I have been a new mama.

With sleepless nights and spit-up covered clothes.

Walking around clueless and dazed and overwhelmed with joy and fear, in equal measure.

I have been a toddler mama.

Chasing and chasing and chasing.

Listening to "watch this!" on repeat.

Trying to break all the falls and clean all the messes and sneak all the snuggles.

I have been an adolescent mama.

Watching toys become a thing of the past and eye contact being replaced by eye-rolling.

Painting bedrooms in "grown-up" colors and bagging up outgrown clothing.

I have been a teenage mama.

Noting changes in voices and attitudes and bodies.

Stealing hugs and holding on tightly until the hold is broken by the younger person.

Feeling time nipping at the heels of every moment together.

I have been an adult mama.

Hastily answering all phone calls and holding my breath until I'm assured all is well.

Realizing that the rooms in our home feel bigger because furniture has been removed and clothes have been packed away and people have changed addresses ... permanently.

I have been a mama in stages.

I have felt presence as fiercely as absence.

I have known abundant joy and overwhelming grief.

I have held tightly and let go and wiped tears ... many of them mine.

I have wanted so badly to be *not needed*, and I have equally loved being *needed in abundance*.

I have plugged my ears to drown out the chaos, and I have turned down every outside noise to not miss a single syllable.

I have loved with my whole heart and loved with holes in my heart.

I have gripped tightly to every moment, and I have relaxed my hold with each passing day.

I have been humbled and honored and hurt and held.

I have had moments of the euphoric feeling of success, and I have felt the near-capsizing weight of failure.

I have been a mama in stages.

Sometimes it has been with sidesplitting laughter. Sometimes it has been on the floor, on my face, gasping for breath. There is no way to prepare. There are too many variables and too many guidelines and not enough hours in any given day.

Here's what I need you to know:

You will be a mama in stages.

No matter how much you read or prepare or plan or schedule, you will succeed, and you will fail. Not one or the other. Both.

You will laugh, and you will cry.

You will be on the highest peak, and you will sometimes find yourself in the lowest valley.

Sometimes these events will happen on the same calendar day.

You will hold until it hurts, and you will hurt letting go.

You will pray you did enough, and you will still feel inadequate at the end of most days.

You will inhale comparison and exhale frustration, or you will inhale truth and exhale peace.

Some days will be a little of both.

Give grace upon grace upon grace … to your children and to yourself.

Love yourselves, mamas. Love yourselves well.

Tell yourself the truth and reject lies.

You. Are. Enough.

Today, tomorrow, and forever.

In every stage, you always have been, always are, and always will be enough.

Rest in that.

HERE'S WHAT I NEED YOU TO KNOW
{about college}

I t's almost time. The preparation has been underway for weeks.
You purchased happy-colored tote bins. You bought cheap boxes and packing tape. You wandered around Target and Walmart and all the places getting new sheets and towels and washcloths. (You have personally used threadbare sheets for the last ten years, but no child of yours will head off to an institution of higher learning with those old rags.) You stocked up on toiletries and school supplies and all. the. things. You bought the sticky strips and the trash can and the shoe organizer.

If you have a girl, you most likely bought the dangling lights and the coordinating wall decor. She probably picked out the bed linens; you added the throw blanket because she CANNOT HAVE COLD FEET WHILE STUDYING, FOR HEAVEN'S SAKE!

If you have a boy, you probably talked him into new sheets and a rug to put alongside the bed. You made him promise to do laundry once a week, and you showed him how to use the washing machine, even though you secretly hope he will show up after the first week of school with all his dirty laundry in tow for you to do for him.

Some of you watched the packing.

Some of you were invited to help.

Into the suitcase went their old-faithful clothing items, the ones you have seen all too often on their bodies and in their dirty laundry. You recommended air freshener and extra socks and a winter coat; because YOU NEVER KNOW WHEN A COLD FRONT WILL BLOW IN!

They bypass extra sweaters, and because you know they will wish they had them, you snuck them into their things when they weren't looking. They either packed too much or packed too little; either way, your heart hurt.

With every fold, you felt the years being wrapped up. The click of the storage bin lids and the zipping of the suitcases were signals to you both: We will leave here one way and arrive back ... different. There's no going back to "before" exactly as it stands.

You have tried to prepare yourself. You have had many years to anticipate this event, and yet ... your mind has been like the tide, thoughts quietly ebbing and flowing peacefully around one moment, only to find them violently crashing on top of one another the very next.

One second you feel overprepared only to suddenly remember that you have forgotten so many things.

What your words say is: "Do you have enough?" But what your heart says is: "Have I done enough?"

You will load the cars and travel the miles and carry all the boxes and bins, wondering how anyone does this four years in a row.

You will watch them unpack, and if you are really lucky, they will let you hang things up or put things in the dresser drawers.

You will watch them walk away a final time or close the dorm room door, and you will fight back tears and sadness indistinguishable from your pride and respect, and it will all mesh into one big, messy smile that you plaster on your face.

Here's what I need you to know:

"Enough," in this case, is a figment of our imaginations. It is an unattainable goal with standards set by people who play no part in our lives. It is a mirage and a trap and a bottomless pit.

You did all you knew to do.

You hugged and held and dried tears and bandaged wounds.

You pointed out the silver lining and always found the moral of every story.

You cheered the loudest no matter what the accomplishment, and you picked up the pieces when life was falling apart.

Every day was a lesson for you both.

And now, when it's time to watch them start over in a new place, this is what I can assure you: They will still need you. They will still call you. They will still value your relationship, and they will love you even more than you ever thought they did.

Because distance gives perspective, and absence makes ALL the hearts grow fonder, not just yours.

They will leave as your children, and they will return at winter break as your friends.

They will call you for advice, and they will sometimes even take it.

They will want you to come see them, and they will be so proud to show you their new lives.

Loosen your grip, mamas.

When we let go of them, it allows us to spread our arms even wider for them when they come back. And they do come back.

They come back stronger and smarter and with *lots* of dirty laundry.

HERE'S WHAT I NEED YOU TO KNOW
{about knowing your part}

Both of my boys have played football at some point in their lives. The oldest boy, who is tall and thin, decided early on that it wasn't the sport for him. He used to get in his position on the field, and it all looked great to my inexperienced eye. After each game, though, he would tell me, "Mom, I don't like getting hit." I knew that was mostly what football seemed to be about, so we ushered him into other hobbies and sports.

It came as no surprise when his younger brother was old enough to voice his opinion that he wanted to be a football player like his big brother had been. We signed him up and suited him up and shuffled him to and from practices and games. He's old enough to drive himself now, and he still loves the sport with a passion.

This kid looks the part. He is a tall, strapping boy-man. He is comfortable throwing and catching and tackling and blocking. Once a week during football season, he makes his mama's heart half stop as he stands face-to-face with other boy-men. Some of them are smaller, and some are larger than he is. Regardless, this mama struggles with each play, knowing what the possibilities are. It doesn't matter that he has played most of his life. It still makes me cringe every time the players take the field.

My son has man-size hands and an appetite to match his sturdy, six-foot-four-inch frame. He can grip the ball comfortably and hang on to it for dear life. He played for years with the uniform seeming to hang on his body, and now that he is almost a fully grown man, he fills out the padding and carries himself with confidence. He has played the sport for long enough to be well versed in the game, in particular, the offensive line where he takes his place. He analyzes film. He can quote plays. He is intimidating on the field due to his size alone.

Many times I catch myself pondering my children's lives, as mamas often do. I think about their futures and wonder what life will hand them. I think about who they will fall in love with and what careers they will choose. So it was no surprise that one day recently, I found myself thinking about this middle child of mine and his football obsession. I love that he still loves the game. I love that practice doesn't make him grumble and that he takes pride in his team and in himself.

Out of nowhere, though, this thought occurred to me and has been plaguing my mind ever since: this kid, this boy-man athlete who practices daily, studies the rules, dresses out for every game, and runs the plays and *never* touches the ball in a game!

Like, ever.

Unless he somehow recovers a fumble, his chances are slim to none that he will ever place his fingers on that tough leather in an actual game. I asked him about this because my mom heart wondered how it felt to participate in a game where he had almost zero chance of even grazing his fingers across the most important piece of equipment in the game.

"How does it feel to practice hard, dress the part, show up at game time, run, sweat, listen, follow the plays ... and never touch the ball?" I asked him.

His reply was simple, without fanfare or disappointment or even a hint of frustration. "That's not my job."

His answer caught me completely off guard. I guess deep inside I wanted some righteous indignation to rise up.

I wanted him to *want* to touch the ball, to feel mistreated because he was not getting that chance. I wanted him to want to be catching the passes and running the yards and scoring the points. But I just kept hearing his words in my head: "That's not my job."

Here's what I need you to know:
Most everyone wants to catch the amazing passes and run the field with the wind at their backs, pushing away the obstacles. Everyone wants to score the points and hear the crowd cheer and be recognized for their accomplishments. But it's not everyone's job to do that.

Some of us, like this gentle giant I have raised, are the blockers. We hold the line. We hold back the opposition. We are the ones keeping the opponents at bay so the ball can get through and the points get scored. That means that sometimes we have to watch the ball go by and trust that our fellow teammates do their part, trust that they, too, will play their positions.

If everyone tries to catch every pass and run to the end zone and score every point, what we end up with is a chaotic scene. We end up with collisions and injuries and fumbles. People get hurt, and nothing gets accomplished.

We can learn so much from my son's simple, humble answer. **Some things, simply, are not our job.**

The sooner we recognize this, the sooner we find our place. We settle in. We get good at the position we are in, and as a result, everyone around us succeeds—everyone at our jobs, everyone in our homes, everyone in our friend groups and church groups and play groups.

Whether in your personal life or your professional life or both: **Position is everything. Find your place.**

Learn your role.

Study your part.

And then … watch the winning happen.

HERE'S WHAT I NEED YOU TO KNOW
{about your words}

Twice a year, I work full-time hours at a part-time job, helping to set up and run a seasonal children's consignment sale. It's organized chaos, and aside from motherhood, it is the most fulfilling work I have ever done. We take an empty building, load all our materials in, set up our racks, take in every child-related item known to mankind, inspect every article of clothing, sort through tons and tons of toys and assorted baby and child gear, organize everything, sell most of the items, return the unsold items, donate designated items, and then we tear it all back down again until the next sale. It's exhausting and exhilarating all at the same time.

The work is full time and overtime and all the time. For thirty solid days. When the event is finally set up and sorted out and ready to "open," a collective sigh of relief ripples through the staff. It feels like we have finished, when in reality, we are still only halfway through. Once the sale actually opens, it's full-throttle greeting and assisting and scanning and taking payments. If you're tired after reading all that, you get the general idea.

It's organized chaos ... madness-filled ... pedal to the metal; it's a go, go, go time. Then, almost as quickly as it started, it's over.

A mother came through my checkout line during a recent sale. She was cheerful and happy and toting a newborn in a front carrier. We made small talk. She told me she only had one child, and I assumed it was the baby she was carrying around. When I asked how old he was, she laughed and pointed at the little girl in the stroller, told me the girl was hers, and that she was two years old. Then she said, "She's the only one I have because she's mean. She's bad, and she's hateful and mean. She might look sweet, but she's fooling you. She's evil."

I will honestly admit that I don't really know what message my face delivered. After raising five children, I would like to think I have heard it all and that my face hides what my mind is thinking.

I thought of a lot of things I wanted to say. I thought of a lot of things I wanted to do. But I held my tongue because, let's face it, that's what we do. We turn a blind eye. We tune out, and we carry on, and we remind ourselves that every situation isn't ours to respond to. We do it to keep the peace. Sometimes it's called "looking the other way," and sometimes we call it "minding our own business." Then, I looked at that little girl and I thought: Shame on you, mama, for speaking hateful words about your flesh and blood. Shame on you for standing right beside the gift you've been given and expressing ungratefulness. Shame on you for speaking such words. Ever. And especially shame on you for speaking them right there where she could see you and hear you.

Here's what I need you to know:
Your mouth has the ability to make or break the spirit of your child. Your words have the power to heal and give hope, but they also have the power to clench a tight fist around the spirit of your littles.

If you say your child is mean, I can assure you, you will get a mean child. If you speak words of selfishness and temper and anger over your child, do not rear back in surprise when those words come to life in ways you never even imagined. If you call your child hateful and evil, get ready.

Children are children. They need guidance and love and direction and boundaries. What they need most, however, is hope.

Hope that you believe the good that is within them.

Hope that they are not going to disappoint you.

Hope that even if they do, you will not love them any less.

Hope that you can be trusted to bring out the best from deep within their untamed spirits and show them how to be better than yesterday.

Your words matter, mama.

All of them.

So speak them wisely.

HERE'S WHAT I NEED YOU TO KNOW
{about being in the moment}

My kids started a very bad habit a few years back. Actually, maybe they always had this habit, and I just noticed it then. Regardless, it drove me crazy.

Our family would be enjoying a day, say, at a theme park. I would take a split second to "mom relax" (which isn't *actual* relaxing but is closer to relaxing than not relaxing at all).

Here we would be, taking in all the sights and sounds of said theme park, and one of my littles would say something like, "Mom, do you think maybe next week we could go to the skating rink?"

My reaction was usually something like, "ARE YOU KIDDING ME RIGHT NOW? We are right here, right now, in this theme park! Can you not see the themes [pointing vigorously to the rides and signs and such]? Can you not see the park [pointing hither and yon at benches and trees and other people relaxing]? How could you possibly be asking me to plan another event for another day in another place when you can't even enjoy this one! Stop complaining and enjoy this day, darn it!"

I'm not proud of that reaction, but it was what it was.

Then, my life took a drastic turn. Some of that redirection was due to choices I had made; I was in a cycle of selfishness and self-pity. Some was due to the choices of others. Often, the people we love the most cause us the most hurt. Regardless, I found myself in a situation that shifted my thinking, forcing me to decide if I was going to keep bumping into the corners of the past or embrace the here and now.

Hindsight is often said to be 20/20, and while I do not totally disagree with that, I think there is more to be said …

Looking back at a situation isn't a bad idea, but staring back and not looking away *is*. That little rearview mirror in our vehicles is little for a reason. It's a place of reflection (pun free and completely intended) and a viewpoint to gather a sense of our surroundings, but it is *not* there for us to stare at and focus on. That kind of looking back shields our view forward and leaves the potential for accidents. In life, when we look back, rarely do we say, "I'm so glad I made that decision," or "That was the day things changed for the better." Usually, we look back and focus on what might have been or what went drastically wrong. We rarely see what went beautifully right.

Hindsight tends to be 20/20 because it is easy to see when you know exactly what you're looking for. Hidden pictures with no list of items to find are brutal, but give me those little images that let me know what specifically I am looking for, and I am golden.

I am also convinced that focusing *only* forward can be just as tragic. Sometimes we spend so much time on our expectations of how we *think* things should be and what we *expect* to happen that we totally miss the events happening right around us at that very moment.

And when life does not line up with our expectations, as it rarely ever does, we live in a constant state of disappointment, always looking around us for the next thing. The next event. The next plan.

Here's what I need you to know:
When we are doing something as a family or spending time at some event, and my kids come to me and ask about something at a future date or want to talk about something we used to do, I always tell them, **"Let's just be in this moment."**

I have said it so many times now that most of the time when they even start to ask, they pause, realizing what is going to come out of my mouth next. They often don't bother to even finish the question.

"Let's just be in this moment." I don't elaborate. I don't give reasons why. It is a simple phrase to redirect us back to the moment. It has become a beautiful thing.

The world is such a busy place, and we are such busy people. Following this mantra—let's just be in *this* moment—has given me such a victory. It gives me permission to just enjoy where we are right at that very moment. Not thinking about the future, not thinking about the past, just living in the here and now.

It is not about never planning or never anticipating or never hoping for good things to happen. It is just simply about not living as a prisoner to our schedules.

This learning to just be is a beautiful thing. It slows time and releases anxiety, and it brings expectations into focus.

Try it.

Just be in the moment.

You will not regret it.

HERE'S WHAT I NEED YOU TO KNOW
{about marriage}

This year, my husband and I will celebrate another year of marriage.

This year ... we will celebrate.

Some years, we have marked the passage of time.

These are *not* the same thing.

Sometimes, an anniversary is a celebration, and sometimes, let's be honest, it's just a way to commemorate another trip around the sun.

If you've been married more than ten years, I think you might agree that weddings are easy, and marriage is hard. For years, around our anniversary, I would tell friends as long as no one had died or had an affair, it was a year to celebrate.

And then, what we had always said would *never* happen happened. Right when we thought we had this marriage thing conquered.

Want to know what twenty-seven-plus years of marriage looks like? It looks like smiles and laughter, vacations and memories. It looks like home projects and child-rearing, college tuition and car payments. It looks like moving houses and changing jobs and getting raises and achieving promotions ...

Here's what I need you to know:
Marriage also looks like clenched fists and tightened jawlines. It looks like hurt feelings and crushed dreams. Marriage looks like failed plans and disappointments, self-loathing and masquerading.

But, when done well, it mostly looks like hurt bathed in forgiveness. Anger enveloped in mercy. It looks like holding your tongue and uncrossing your arms. It looks like stepping back and leaning in and turning a deaf ear to the world. It looks like holding on and letting go. It looks like pushing through and hanging back. It looks like waiting and trusting and believing.

Marriage looks like hostility and humility shaking hands. It looks like compromise and companionship, like giving out and giving in and giving up and giving over. It looks like holding your hands to the fires of life and praying no one gets burned. It looks like stoking the embers even if the flames seem to have disappeared.

Sometimes, it looks like beauty from ashes. When you can look back, accept what has been, embrace what is, and look forward to what will be ... that ... that is a successful marriage.

The world may tell you to walk away. Give up. Start over. But it's in the holding fast ... *the hanging on* ... the weight-carrying, gut-wrenching, heart-hurting moments, that oneness comes.

And when that is your legacy, you celebrate.

HERE'S WHAT I NEED YOU TO KNOW
{about anxiety in teenagers}

As I have done every semester that I've had a child in high school, I recently headed over to get my kid out of class and traipsed into the counselor's office to come up with an Individual Graduation Plan for the upcoming semester.

I remember going to the counselor in my own high school exactly *one* time and getting exactly *zero* information. I headed into every semester (and especially into college) very overwhelmed and scared of the future. How I graduated with all the requirements I needed is a miracle of the highest proportion. That sense of not really knowing what needed to be done was a feeling I did not want my own littles to experience. I think it is okay to shelter them from some things.

So there we were, the guidance counselor, my soon-to-be eleventh grader, and myself. We sat down at the desk and began the process of lining up what classes my middle boy wanted to take the following year. His choices amazed me: English 3 Honors … Algebra 2 Honors … Chemistry Honors … French 3 Honors (because he's undecided about colleges, and he wants to be sure to have all three years of foreign language … just in case). He asked to declare his "major" as hospitality and tourism, and he chose culinary arts as an elective underneath that major.

Then he asked if he could take agriculture science and then specifically asked to take Advanced Placement US history. Finally, he asked if he still had room for driver's ed, because duh ...

He made his own choices, and he aimed higher than I ever imagined.

We signed all the paperwork, and he headed back to class and I to work. All was right in the world ... until it wasn't.

Two hours after our meeting, the same boy of mine texted me: "I think I'm having an anxiety attack. What do I do?"

I am sure I literally stopped in my tracks. Had I not *just* spent half an hour or more sitting shoulder to shoulder with this kid? Had he not actively participated in selecting his own classes? He seemed just fine. What on earth could possibly be causing him anxiety?

I told him to skip football, and I drove to school forty-five minutes early. I parked my car right outside the doors of the school like the crazy mamas. I told him exactly where to find me as if he were five years old, and it was the first day of kindergarten. And then I waited, almost holding my breath to hear the final bell and see his precious face.

He got in the car with me, and I asked the hard questions. (Parents, do not skip the hard questions. It is tempting, but ask them anyway.)

He started responding by saying he had mountains of homework (probably due to missing almost a week of school the week before from strep throat), but then the floodgates opened. He was exhausted from football practice; he wasn't sure he wanted to continue in the chorus next year; he was overwhelmed with playing AAU basketball ... and learning to drive ... and having no "free" time ... and sometimes his friends were jerks ...

The list seemed endless.

My heart was breaking.

He was silent afterward, and I tried to be respectful of the personal space he needed, even though we were a mere two feet apart.

When I finally stole a glance in his direction, my six-foot-four, 195-pound fifteen-year-old son had tears streaming down his face.

I was undone.

This was not the child I knew. This was not the boy I had lived with for the last fifteen years. This did not even remotely resemble the boy I had just sat shoulder to shoulder with in the guidance counselor's office as we received, well, guidance.

All I could think of was that this is how a child becomes a statistic … and I felt my heart shred at the thought of watching my child fall down the rabbit hole of anxiety and depression—and possibly worse.

We have done all the parenting things:

He has a bedtime … even on the weekends.

He doesn't play video games on school nights.

He is expected to help with the pets and keep his room presentable.

He is all things typical and well-rounded. He is athletic and charming, smart and witty, talented and driven.

We have *done* all the things, and he *is* all the things …

And yet …

He is sad.

In a matter of moments, I found myself trying to access in my brain every piece of advice I had ever read to help an overwhelmed person. I was hearing all the quotes. I was running all the statistics through my head. I was determined to find a way to talk him off the proverbial ledge because in my mind, the next logical step was that he would be on a real ledge, and *that* did not happen to families like ours.

This is where your mind goes when all logic and reason seem illogical and unreasonable. I wanted to channel my inner Brené Brown and come up with some earth-shaking words of wisdom that would forever change the trajectory of his life and that people would want to post and repost on Pinterest under boards called "Inspiration" or "Words of Wisdom."

These are the only sentences I could string together though: "Son, I love you. It's my job to help you through every phase of life, and this is just that … a phase of life. Some of it may suck, but there's still good in every day to be had. We will find it together, and I'll always be on your side."

I sounded like every cliché I had ever heard. There was nothing earth-shattering or prizewinning about my words. But it was all I had.

Here's what I need you to know:
Life is hard. Growing up is hard. There are things that are simply rites of passage as our littles age. That's understood, but ...

I will cancel all the plans and forego all the "things" and simplify the world around my people to whatever extent is necessary if it means saving their lives.

Hug your kids. Say the words, "I love you." (Don't assume they know or feel it.) And listen, listen, listen. Sometimes what is *not* being said is what really needs to be heard. Ask all the hard questions—and be willing to hear all the hard answers.

He texted me later on: "Thank you for listening to me. It really means a lot."

That night I stayed awake and watched him sleep as if he were a newborn. And the next day, I reminded him how very much I loved him—over and over and over again—so he had no doubt, and I reminded him that we will always be in this thing together.

I am mostly, though, just going to learn to listen.

HERE'S WHAT I NEED YOU TO KNOW
{about assigned seating}

Recently, I was at the airport, waiting to catch the final leg of a trip home from California. I was emotionally exhausted from leaving my biggest girl, knowing in a matter of hours I would be over two thousand miles away, and I was physically exhausted from a hectic week spent cramming all the memories we could into my time with her on *her* coast.

My first flight had no Wi-Fi (I know, petty), but I was looking forward to uninterrupted movie watching. My only in-flight goal was to stay distracted enough to somehow forget I was heading *away* from one of my people. When the plane landed, I raced to grab food because I was so hungry, I was getting irritable, and then I raced to the gate. I plugged in my phone to charge, settled into a chair, and began to quickly eat my breakfast/lunch/dinner.

That's the exact moment I received a text that my flight had changed gates, and *right then* I needed to unplug my phone, pack my food up, and race to another gate of unknown location. *Of course.*

When I finally came to a screeching halt at the new gate, literally just at the time boarding was supposed to start, I heard over the intercom that our flight was delayed due to a "technical difficulty" (which turned out to be no air-conditioning and STILL wasn't fixed for the two-hour, forty-five-minute flight home, but I digress). Again, I plugged my phone in to charge, settled into a chair, unpacked my food, and ate as I waited.

And waited.

And waited some more.

Realizing I might be there awhile, I did what many people do when surrounded by lots of people filled with lots of time: I listened.

The people across from me were discussing their travel plans. The people beside me were discussing food. The conversation that caught my attention, though, was the one going on behind me because they were all discussing their seat assignments on the plane.

Someone was in 20A.

Someone was in 20B.

Someone was in 24A.

They talked about aisle seats versus window seats, and they were truly stressing that they would not all be sitting together.

It was about this time that I noticed my own seat assignment: 20C.

I had bought the cheapest ticket with no seat assignment until check-in, so I honestly didn't care where I sat. I was missing my girl and was ready to see my family and just wanted a seat. Any seat.

I was on the verge of turning around to tell this family that I would give up my seat so they could all sit together when I heard one of them say, "I am in 20C."

What?

How was that even possible? I was looking at my boarding pass, and my seat was 20C. The seat was mine. *Mine.*

I went from the woman willing to give up her seat so a family could stay united to Airport Karen faster than a child newly dressed for a snowy adventure outside needs to pee. My flesh began to rise up. I could feel my face getting flushed. I gripped that boarding pass—the one with *my* seat clearly labeled on it—so tightly my fingers nearly lost their circulation.

These people had *no idea* what I had been through to get to this point. They had *no idea* that my nerves were shot, and I was leaving half my heart on this coast while heading across the country, *and* my last flight hadn't had Wi-Fi. (That last part still felt like an important detail.)

I was nearly at the point of turning around to address the family that now was, in my opinion, the enemy. I am usually anticonfrontation to a fault.

Cold food at a restaurant? I'll deal with it.

Slow drivers in the left lane? I'll just go around them.

This time, though, things felt different. Seat 20C was *mine*, and I wasn't giving it up. My sense of generosity was gone. My selfishness took over. Try and take my seat, strangers. Just. Try. It.

And then I heard: "The board at least shows now that we are headed to Miami. They finally got that right."

Miami?

I was headed for Charlotte.

This I knew.

What I did not know or pay attention to in my seat-protecting fog was that I had inadvertently seated myself right between two gates. In my haste to take care of myself, I hadn't even considered that those around me might *not* be trying to take my seat, they actually might not even be on the same plane as me.

I immediately felt ashamed.

Why did I automatically assume that someone was trying to take something that was mine? Why did I assume that there couldn't possibly be enough seats to go around? That somehow this person had managed to get my assigned seat, regardless of what the paper in my hand stated? I realized, in that moment, that this is what we do.

We assume that if someone gets a new house, we will never have a new house.

We assume that if someone receives a job promotion, we will never rise through the ranks of our company.

We assume that if someone has beautiful lashes, ours will somehow be less than beautiful, or if someone makes a fantastic meal, we are basically cooking from the microwave.

Somehow, we have decided that there isn't enough stuff or blessings or prosperity or friendship or love or on and on and on to go around. Someone has to win, and someone has to lose. Someone gets it all, and someone gets nothing.

We cave in on ourselves and feel "less than" and decide, of our own free will, that we will never measure up. No one tells us that. We just decide it ourselves.

Here's what I need you to know:
That thought process is a lie. **Our prosperity or blessing or gift or talent is never dependent on what those around us have.** Sometimes that blessing is due to favor. Sometimes it is due to hard work. But never, under any circumstances, are those blessings limited to a specific quantity.

We can celebrate the grace bestowed on others and still live in expectation of our own grace. **We can simultaneously be rooting for our neighbor's success while still being expectant of our own blessings.** So let's cheer each other on. Let's make a habit of seeing our neighbor prosper and being grateful *for* them, all while still living in a state of thankfulness and assurance that we, too, are worthy of all things good.

Let's remember that everyone isn't out to take our seat on the plane.

HERE'S WHAT I NEED YOU TO KNOW
{about pruning}

I saw this tree the other day. It was all cut back, the branches short and bluntly clipped off at the ends. It looked quite stark in comparison to its usual flowery beauty. I'm sure that it could have been perceived as being dead ... or at the very least, unhealthy. It seemed desolate and lonely ... like it had lost its way in the midst of the surrounding chaos. I wondered if people could remember what it looked like in all its full-bloom glory. Did people understand that it would not be stripped of its beautiful color and greenery forever?

Did casual observers understand that it was trimmed close on purpose? Was it clear that the unnecessary and dead and overgrown parts had to be cut away in order for the tree to increase its fullness and growth?

I wonder if you see that's what's happening in you.

Maybe you had to pack up your life.

Maybe you had to move from your home or your job or your comfort.

Maybe you had to let go of a dream.

Maybe you lost your purpose.

Maybe you had to accept a diagnosis.

Maybe you had to rescue an addict or ask for help or suffer unimaginable loss.

Maybe just getting out of bed is all you can do today.

Maybe the ground you stood so firmly on has shifted in such a significant way that you wonder if it is even still there.

Perhaps, in this moment, your life feels bluntly clipped off. Maybe others see starkness in comparison to your usual flowery beauty. Sometimes you seem desolate and lonely, like you have lost your way in the midst of the surrounding chaos.

Here's what I need you to know:
It won't be this way forever. You are being shaped this way for a purpose.

Trust me when I tell you that what is happening is the intentional and selective removal of certain parts of your life for the purpose of controlling and redirecting your growth, improving and sustaining your health, and increasing the yield and quality of your future growth.

Some of the process is painful. Some of it is ugly. Some of it seems unnecessary to the casual observer, but each and every part of it is for your good and your growth.

Hang on. Keep your eyes on the destination. All the steps won't feel steady. Some will be hard to make out, and often, you will have to stop and gather yourself and get your bearings.

Pruning leads to new growth and new life and new beauty. The end result is beautiful, but it can feel desolate in the middle. The cutting away hurts, but the new growth is so worth it.

So be shapeable. Be patient. Allow yourself to be pruned. Extend grace to your neighbor when they seem sharp and blunt. Maybe they, too, are being pruned. The process might hurt, but what will grow after that process will be amazing.

HERE'S WHAT I NEED YOU TO KNOW
{about phones at the table}

Recently, when our family was eating at a restaurant, I noticed a family nearby with no one looking at a phone. I quickly glanced around our table. All of us, and I mean all seven of us, were using our phones.

Here's what else I noticed: The table without the phones was silent. There wasn't a single word of conversation going on. In fact, the people sitting there weren't even looking directly at each other. (I did notice some sideways glances of disapproval, probably for us all being on our phones.)

Now, I realize there could be an infinite number of reasons for the silence.

Maybe they had been forced to put their phones away.

Maybe they all just had a big argument before coming out to eat, and no one felt like talking.

Maybe they had experienced a recent death in the family or some other tragedy that rendered them speechless.

Maybe all of the above applied or maybe none of the above.

I looked back at my table. The three guys were all comparing Fantasy football decisions and stats. They were making trades and trying to con each other into making deals. They were serious one second and laughing the next.

The girls were looking through recent photos they had taken and sharing their experiences with each other. They were giggling and smiling and clearly loving every second of it.

I, myself, was coloring a picture on an app.

Was it mindless? Yes.

Was it juvenile? Yes.

Was I loving every second of it? Yes.

Here's what I need you to know:

Maybe we have it all wrong in our family. Maybe we should always, at every meal, put our phones away (which is always the rule when we eat at our table at home).

Maybe we should have forced conversation or awkward moments of intermittent silence when we have nothing to talk about.

Maybe we should hold more sacred the time we have around the table together as a family. It is rare these days.

But maybe, just maybe, we have it just right. **Maybe what's most important is that we are communicating and sharing.** Maybe the laughs and jokes and smiles and conversations are exactly what our family needs. Maybe, through the endless things we can do with our phones, we are opening up lines of communication and topics of conversation that might never arise naturally.

Maybe, just maybe, when it comes to whether phones are allowed at tables, either at home or at restaurants, we could mind our own business. Maybe we could find what works for us and use it.

Maybe we could stop pointing fingers and making judgment calls about situations we have no knowledge of or control over, and we could just focus on our own people.

I'm pretty convinced that we all have more to deal with than to worry about our neighbor's phone habits.

HERE'S WHAT I NEED YOU TO KNOW
{about leaving home}

I watched you pack tonight. I watched you try and gather as much of "home" as you could cram into those two large suitcases, and while you compressed clothing and necessities, my heart was compressing every moment since your birth into memories.

I want to remember it all. I want to collect every moment we have shared and bottle it up like champagne so we can open it up with a loud burst when you return and spend the evening saying, "Remember when …"

And yet even as I watch you, I know there are things I have already forgotten. So very many things my mind cannot access anymore.

I want to chase after you as you walk away from me at the airport, reminding you to look both ways before you cross the street and to not talk to strangers and to pay attention to your surroundings. I want to cover you in full body armor and wrap your heart in bubble pack and whisper to you that everyone in this world is not nice but that everyone needs love.

Here's what I need you to know:
All people need love. Even the unkind people. Especially the unkind ones.

I want to remind you of all the truth I've ever told you and all the Bible verses you ever learned, and I want to hug your heart tightly and remind you that grace is unmerited, but so needed by the world.

I want you to be able to feel my heart across the miles.

I want you to hear my voice inside you when the world lets you down and things don't go as planned.

Mostly, I want you to know how very brave I think you are.

Go with my blessing. Chase after all that is adventurous and beautiful and look wide-eyed at it all ... soak it all in ... breathe in every second of this amazing journey. We will be here when you come home, and we will share those memories and stories along with what I know will be many new ones.

You are loved.

You are smart.

You. Are. Enough.

Now it's time to go show the world what all of us here already know. May you feel the love across the miles from all of us who have been chapters in your story thus far, and may the new chapters you write continue to tell a most beautiful story.

Sharpen your pencil, child of mine. Grab your notebook and turn to a fresh page. We have been writing the introduction for years now. It's finally time for you to take over the story.

Here's to many more beautiful chapters yet unwritten.

HERE'S WHAT I NEED YOU TO KNOW
{about taking risks)

This story is for ladies. Ladies of a certain age, maybe midthirties and later. If this does not apply to you, feel free to skip on over to another chapter. If you stay, I cannot promise that you will not be scarred for life.

The previous words will serve as the disclaimer for the words that follow.

Let me start by saying this: I do not take full responsibility for the outcome of this story. I was framed. Pure and simple. This was a set up from the start, and I will never believe anything less.

Here is the bottom line: sometimes, even your best friends will set you up for a fall, all for laughter's sake. There ... I said it.

Years ago, while I was in what I know now were my younger years, I attended a discipleship weekend. It was designed to be a long weekend— one of those Thursday evening through early Sunday deals. Several girlfriends and I crammed our necessities into bags and ourselves into a rental van and headed for the hills of Tennessee.

This was not just *any* group of ladies. These ladies were the *good* ones. The ones who, if you have decided to attend a discipleship weekend in the hills of Tennessee where you will know no one else, you will want to take along.

The weekend was, by design, very scripted. There were speakers and sessions. Moments of quiet and moments of conversation. It was also, maybe not by design, very cultlike. I say that with great love.

It was indeed *not* a cult gathering ... this I know. But were you to compare a cult gathering to this weekend, I am just saying the similarities would be obvious.

The focus on gaining new members.

Dedicated mealtimes, with no deviation from the schedule.

Discouragement of questioning practices.

Moments of meditation.

Some chanting. Even some speaking in tongues.

I knew the group was *not* a cult, but I am going to say that there were moments I did ponder whether I knew how to send smoke signals or which direction I would run should the moment of escape present itself. Regardless, this is how I came to find myself at a rustic campground in the hills of Tennessee, surrounded by mostly strangers, waiting in line for a meal, and needing to pee. *Badly.*

I warned you.

Now, let me assure you—there were restroom facilities. That was not the issue.

The issue was I *love* food. All the foods. All the categories. Count me in for everything.

But with mealtimes being so rigidly scheduled, both starting and ending at a very specific time, I did not want to waste any of that time getting out of line to go to the bathroom. So as any woman in her midthirties who has birthed five children should never do, I decided to wait. The meal line moved quickly, and before I knew it, we had gone through the line, found a table, eaten our fill, and headed back outside to walk up the large, gravel hill to our cabin, therefore bypassing the bathroom.

I knew I was testing the boundaries of a very battered bladder. I knew it was risky walking all the way up that hill, having been filled to the brim for more than an hour ... but I was young and ignorant.

So I told the gals that it would be no problem to wait until we topped the hill and arrived at the cabin.

I didn't know then what I know now about bladders in women in their midthirties. I didn't take into consideration that it was February. I also didn't *for one second* think that someone in the holy group of women I had surrounded myself with would exclaim, as we walked out into the winter evening, "It's so cold my nipples could cut glass." That's it.

That's all it took.

I tried everything not to laugh.

I thought of dead puppies and funerals and every manner of sad thought I could muster up. I held off for a bit with just a small snicker. However, if you have ever been in a group of middle-aged women, on a retreat, in the mountains of Tennessee in the dead of winter, well, you know how well my plan held up.

My snicker became a chuckle, and my chuckle slid over into a laugh, which in just a matter of seconds became a full-on hysterical fit.

And that was *all it took* for my bladder to remind me who was in charge.

I would like to say that the damage was minimal.

A small trickle, maybe?

Alas, that was not to be.

Standing there in the mountains of Tennessee, at the bottom of that gravel hill, already needing to pee, I tempted fate with laughter, and fate took home the trophy. In a matter of seconds, I went from responsible thirtysomething to preschool toddler.

I was soaked.

I don't mean change-your-drawers damp.

I don't mean maybe-someone-might-notice wet.

I mean full-on, standing-in-an-ever-growing-puddle-soaked-through-a-pair-of-denim-blue-jeans soggy.

And guess who, for the sake of "packing lightly" had only brought one singular pair of jeans for the weekend?

This woman right here.

The one standing in a puddle of her own wee-wee.

I do not remember much else about that fateful weekend. I know someone from "the camp" took my clothes to be laundered while I lounged around in my pajamas. I know when I reemerged from my shameful hideout, I was greeted with hugs and laughter and the most oddly authentic love from friends I have ever felt. I also know that I learned never to trust even a partially full bladder in the dead of winter, in the mountains of Tennessee, at the bottom of a gravel hill, while walking with a group of friends. *Never.*

Here's what I need you to know:
Humiliation and acceptance are often close cousins.

I am convinced we often forfeit great growth when we refuse to laugh at ourselves.

Let it go, ladies. **Be a risk taker even if things don't end well.**

Those moments always become the stories of legacies.

HERE'S WHAT I NEED YOU TO KNOW
{about the FAFSA}

There are some givens in life if you have children who plan to attend college: You will be born. You will die. You will have to fill out the Federal Application for Federal Student Aid (FAFSA). If you don't know what that is, you are either independently wealthy, you have been out of college for so long that you have forgotten, you never needed it because you opted out of college, or your parents did it for you.

Assuming that most parents are like myself and will fill out the financial aid form *for* the student *each and every* time, I have composed a step-by-step guide to filling out the FAFSA.

1. **Ask your child which college(s) she would like to attend.**
   This will elicit one of two responses:
   a) She will proudly proclaim the college that has always been her dream to attend (if this is the case, skip to step 2).
   b) She will blankly stare at you, as if you are speaking a foreign language.
   Expect that second response. Then wait for what feels like your entire lifetime (but will really be more like three to four minutes). Remind your child that college is the next step after graduation, which is in a few months. Should no response be given, just randomly choose the college(s) of your choice.

Hope you wanted to be a chef, kiddo.

Tough loss. You had your chance.

2: **Have the proper documents handy.** You will need your child's social security card. Yes, I know you haven't seen it since his birth or when he filled out his first job application. You vaguely remember last seeing it when he got a driving permit.

Check the fireproof box that holds all the family's official documents. This seems logical, therefore you should not expect it to be there. Next, check the desk drawers in the living room. Check them all. One drawer will hold all the missing items you have been looking for with the exception of the social security card. Finally, check the random junk drawer that holds all the stuff no one wants to deal with. It will probably be in there.

If not, set up an appointment at the social security office to obtain a new one. Take with you to the appointment the child, your wallet containing an ID, some form of payment, some Harry Potter magic spells, and the patience of a homeschooling mom.

You will need all these things.

After dealing with the social security card issue, make sure you also have your most recent tax return, recent bank statements, and the blood of a thousand goats. If the IRS asks for a tax return from two years ago, don't even question why they want that one. Just find it. If you cannot find any of these items, repeat the process of Step 2, looking again in all the usual places. Yes, you could look for all these items at once, but it is much more realistic if you find each item separately and drag the process out for much longer than should be humanly possible or necessary. This is the voice of experience talking, remember. You should be ready now.

3: **Log on to the FAFSA site.** Just look it up online. Save it as a bookmark on your computer's browser. Then delete it. Trust me—someone else will do it for you if you do not. Each time you save the site for easy reference, "not me" will remove it. You know? The same "not me" that does all the other unwanted things around the house? It might as well be you.

Once you are on the site, you will need to create a Federal Student Aid ID (FSA ID). This will involve a username and a password. Maybe just use the same one you use for everything else. If you're feeling adventurous, get creative with it. Make sure you include an uppercase letter, a number, a symbol, one character in another color, and something in hieroglyphics. If you want, write these things down on a notepad or note on your phone.

Please note that if you use the notepad you leave on the counter for convenience—the one that is always there for messages and important notes—it'll be nowhere to be found when you need it.

If you leave a note on your phone, label the note so you know where to find the information later. I suggest calling the note: THIS IS THE LOGIN INFORMATION FOR THE FAFSA ACCOUNT. Just for the sake of clarity.

On your note, record the username and password you created. Do this within one to two minutes of its creation or plan to start over. (If you have a college-age kid, this is about how long it will take you to forget something you just did.)

4: Start the actual application process.

You have nine months during which you can complete the financial aid application process. Feel free to take breaks, grab a snack, travel, or grow a baby inside you. Just know that the longer you take, the longer it'll take to get financial aid, and the greater the number of times you will forget your password and username and have to reset them.

Every.

Single.

Time.

You.

Log.

On.

The notebook will be nowhere to be found, and the note on your phone will have been deleted. Trust me on this.

5: Follow the prompts and answer the questions asked. This will include, but may not be limited to:

    a.) Your child's name, age, high school attended, and various other personal questions.

    b.) Your name, address, and marriage status.

    c.) Your mother's maiden name, all the places she lived from birth until the age of twenty-one, her favorite book, the last known phone number for her, and her natural hair color.

    d.) Your email address (one that you can access … hope you wrote that password down somewhere as well.)

    e.) Lots of other seemingly useless (yet apparently very important) information.

Then you have to submit your financial information. You can usually access the IRS online and connect your tax records directly to the FAFSA. As with most government agencies, this usually only takes about sixteen tries, three phone calls, and nine or so curse words.

Record how many attempts it takes you to successfully finish and see if you can beat them next fall. Make a challenge out of it.

Sign your name.

Click submit.

Your internet will probably crash at this exact moment in time. Hope you created that save key that allows you to start back where you left off.

Now, just wait for the government to let the school of your child's choice (or yours if your child never did answer) know how much assistance will be given by the federal government.

Here's what I need you to know:

Get a second or third job. **The aid you receive will be way less than you anticipated due to the government deciding you are too wealthy for much aid.**

Don't email them a picture of your mortgage or your pantry.

They don't care.

HERE'S WHAT I NEED YOU TO KNOW
{about what your wife wants for Christmas}

Gentlemen, I am fully aware that we may not currently be anywhere near Christmas. I am with you on this. But for the sake of relationships all across the country, I'm going to go ahead and tell you what your wife wants for Christmas.

She wants her car cleaned out. She doesn't really even care if it actually gets washed. She just wants the inside cleaned.

She wants to be able to reach behind the seat for her purse and not get a handful of month-old French fries, one dirty sock, and a cup of spoiled milk. She wants to be able to drop off the kids at school without the fear of what might potentially fall out when the door opens.

She doesn't care if you pay someone to detail it, you run it through the six-dollar wash at Sam's Xpress, or you clean it yourself in the driveway on a Sunday afternoon. She just wants it cleaned out.

And she wants you to fix that motor in the door of her vehicle that currently keeps her from being able to adjust the side mirrors. Yes, the one on the driver's side door that she told you about six months ago. She needs to be able to adjust that mirror so she can glare at Karen creeping up on her rear bumper in the carpool line.

She needs eye contact. *This is very important.*

She wants her nails done. And she doesn't want you to hand her cash and tell her to "make an appointment" because she won't. Book her an appointment. Go pay for it. Bring her proof in the form of an appointment card and a gift-card receipt. On the rare occasion she treats *herself* to the "nail place," she always feels like she must choose between having hands ready for the Home Shopping Network or beach-ready feet. Don't make her choose between needing gloves or socks. Soft hands *and* feet make for a happy mommy.

Give her both this holiday season.

She wants a facial. You might have to be a little sneaky with this one. Don't just say, "Hey, honey, I got you a facial." This may be misinterpreted. It needs to come disguised as a very large gift card to a great spa with many services offered. She will choose the facial.

Don't go cheap on this one. Her face has been bearing the burdens of the sun, age, makeup, and all the facial responses she has made to your children. She's had the Mona Lisa smile on and eyes rolling into the back of her head taking care of your family for so long, she needs to know she's not permanently stuck that way. She has been using cheap face wipes and slapping on drugstore moisturizer in a desperate attempt to keep from looking like the Crypt Keeper.

Help a mother out.

She wants a weekend away. Sorry, boys, not a weekend away with you. A weekend away with the girls.

Remember that time you went fishing for four days with "play money" and "limited cell phone service"? That.

She wants that. With the girls.

Beach? Mountains? The middle of the nearest body of water? It matters not. Somewhere out there is a rental complete with unlimited adult beverages and clean sheets.

Taking care of the kids and keeping the house running is her life every day, all year long. You can keep everyone alive for four consecutive days.

She wants a Target gift card. This needs no further explanation.

For bonus points, include a Starbucks card so she can enjoy a beverage while she shops.

She wants you to schedule date nights. Regularly. Like you used to do when you dated her and wanted to be in more than just the friend zone.

Hire a babysitter. Don't make your wife choose a restaurant, a movie, or a time to leave. Set it all up and tell her when to be ready.

She wants you to tell her she is beautiful … but not when she is all dressed up for a special event. She wants you to tell her when she is knee-deep in laundry and dinner ingredients.

She wants you to tell her when she is done being creative with the children and sick and tired of picking things up off the floor.

She needs to know that you remember who she is on the inside and that she is still desired, even with her hair up in a bun on a Tuesday afternoon.

Here's what I need you to know:

Ladies, let's face reality. You're the ones reading this book. So make a copy of this chapter. Subtly place it inside his favorite magazine or the bathroom reader, or tape it to the television during Monday Night Football.

You deserve all these things and more. Let's make sure he knows it.

HERE'S WHAT I NEED YOU TO KNOW
{about how I knew}

I know once I'm gone, you'll ask yourself. You'll wonder silently in your head, and you'll wonder out loud to people close to your heart. You'll search over and over for ways you might have known. You'll stay up late into the night asking yourself countless questions. You'll walk through a normal day and then, out of nowhere, you will face-plant into a memory, and there it will be again.

And you'll wonder.

So I want you to know here and now: **I knew.**

I knew by the way you dialed my number first when you had great news.

I knew by the way you texted me pictures of your food and your outfits and your friends.

I knew by the way you stopped by the house—long after you moved away from home—just because you wanted to see everyone. Even after you moved out of town and had to pack a bag and stay overnight, I knew.

I knew by your hugs and your smiles and your laughter—I always knew by your laughter.

Here's what I need you to know:
I also knew in so many other ways.

I knew by the way you slammed the door when we argued. That's how you told me: *this matters to me, and you matter to me, and I want you to know both of those things.* I knew by the way your tears came when you told me news that you knew would disappoint me. Those tears said so much. They told me your heart hurt because your words were making my heart hurt.

I knew by the way you vacillated between choosing to vacation with the family that upcoming summer or hang out with friends and their families. If it didn't matter to you, the decision would have been easy.

I knew when you stood face-to-face and toe-to-toe with me, so certain you were right, and you needed me to see things from your perspective.

Even when you were wrong … or mean … or rude. I knew.

I knew when you planned your wedding and included my thoughts into those plans.

I knew when you stared down the barrel of a budget and called for input.

I knew when you paid for my meals when we ate out or when you brought home a special surprise—just because.

I knew you loved me.

Love is patient.

Love is kind.

Love is not jealous or boastful or proud or rude.

Love does not demand its own way.

It is not irritable, and it keeps no record of wrong.

And, sometimes, love is messy.

It is packaged poorly and misjudged and presented in a less-than-stellar way.

But I knew.

My mama heart always knew.

HERE'S WHAT I NEED YOU TO KNOW
{about messes}

I cannot make this stuff up.

After weeks (months?) riding around in my almost-a-biohazard car, I decided I would whip over to the Sam's Xpress car wash and treat my sweet Silver Bullet to a bath. I was aiming for the basic six-dollar wash. The guy at the pay station "assisting" me with selecting my wash spent the better part of two minutes telling me all the benefits of the unlimited wash package. I'm sure I said no at least four times.

Persistent he was, though, and since he still held a fast grip on my debit card, we came to a compromise, and I stepped my wash up a level. He wasn't fully satisfied, but he pressed the necessary buttons anyway and loosened his fingers from my card, and I drove ahead toward the wash entrance.

I enjoyed all six minutes of the wash. I pretended I was in a land far, far away participating in a color run held during a thunderstorm. Listen—I don't get much free time. Sometimes when I do, my fantasies come out a little jumbled. Don't judge.

After my leisurely ride through the automated wash, I pulled over to the vacuums and proceeded to take a layer of dirt off the floor. I'm going to go on record as saying it looked great, and since it had been so long since I had taken the time to clean it, I vowed then and there in front of Sam himself—and the crazy lady at the bay next to me hand drying her entire vehicle—that I would keep it that way.

Because I had twenty-seven and a half minutes to spare before work, I decided to see what Christmas clearance items the local Kirkland's had that I could not live another season without.

Enter the sweet-smelling, cutely packaged Christmas sachet.

I know what a sachet is. I've had similar ones before. So when I found the cute little packet that smelled so wonderfully appealing, I confidently made my way to the register. I paid, left the store, and sat in my car, ready to add some delicious scent to the now clean interior. I looked the thing over, searching for directions. I wanted to be certain that the sachet was meant to actually *be opened*. The packaging advertised its use in the bathroom, vacuum cleaner bag, trash can, closet, under the car seat, and even in gift baskets.

The package stated it was made from recycled paper. It was 100 percent biodegradable. It even contained essential oils, for Pete's sake. I read every. single. word. I couldn't find *anywhere* whether I was supposed to actually open the package or not. No place did it give any directions as to *how* to use it.

Where? Yes.

How? No.

So I did what seemed totally reasonable—opened it and peeked inside.

What I expected to find was a small, mesh drawstring baggie of this Happy Camper scented delight. What I found instead was the equivalent of firepit ashes. Lovely smelling firepit ashes. Needless to say, I was now in a pickle since the package had been opened.

I headed over to the nearest craft store and scoured the wedding section to find myself a small, mesh baggie so I could transfer this ash substance into a suitable holder to get the most out of the smell. I made the purchase, headed back to my car, and proceeded to make the car-freshening, mesh baggie sachet myself.

I held the cute little mesh baggie open while I poured the ashy contents inside … at which point they promptly seeped out from every pore that baggie had.

Onto everything.

Every solitary surface in the front half of my clean car.

There was no way to stop the flow. It was a Pandora's box (bag?) of pure soot. The more I tried to stop the flow, the more flustered I became and the faster it poured. When I finally was able to stop the flow of dust, I looked around at my formerly clean car as well as myself. The whole tableau now resembled a crime scene, complete with fingerprint dust all over.

Here's what I need you to know:

Sometimes we can look all over for the way to properly handle a thing. Or a situation. Or a person. And we can do our best to prepare the scene and have the proper tools and do what seems like the best with what we know. And things might still become a sooty mess.

Don't let the day be ruined by a bad moment. Don't let the current mess negate all the good, clean, successful moments. Everything cleans up in the end. Shake the dust off—literally and figuratively—and move along.

Regret is an abyss. A sinkhole. Quicksand. Don't fall into the trap.

Even when the mess is all over us, we can still come out smelling fresh and clean.

HERE'S WHAT I NEED YOU TO KNOW
{about capturing the moment}

I know it drives you crazy. Everywhere we go and everything we do—I'm there with my phone snapping pictures.

I'm pretty sure you think I haven't missed a moment of your lives. It's all documented.

Every first.

Every try.

Every new thing or new place or new season.

It's all there.

I've taken pictures of places we have been, things we have done, and yes, foods we have shared. Not every photo has been great. Some are blurry. Some have our heads cut off, or our hair's a mess. Some look like they could have been taken by a third-grader.

Here's what I need you to know:
These pictures aren't only for me. They are also for you.

The truth is, I won't always be here. Someday, who knows when, I'll be gone, and these photos, these poorly timed, last-minute, stop-right-now-and-smile-for-the-camera memories, will be all that's left. They will be all you have.

My voice will fade. Foods I've cooked for you will become distant memories. Our favorite songs to belt out in the car will go out of style, and you might not hear them very often. But these photos ... *they will last*. When time has played its tricks on us and veered our paths in separate directions—whether it's while we are both still on this earth or long after—these pictures will be here to take you back.

So smile for the camera. Indulge me. My view of the bigger picture is staggeringly greater than yours.

Time has a way of making our vision clearer and our perception keener.

I am sure I'll continue to stop you at all the wrong moments.

Midswing.

Midbite.

Middive or midwalk or middrive.

This is what midlife feels like.

I am living and loving every moment, and I am so glad you are on this journey with me. I want to remember, yes. But *more importantly,* I don't want *you* to forget.

So smile for the camera.

You'll thank me one day.

HERE'S WHAT I NEED YOU TO KNOW
{about summer break}

I see you, mama.

I see you the week before school starts back, wondering how it can be that yesterday it was the last day of school, and somehow, already, the entire summer has come crashing into right now. I see you with your unfinished list of things to do. I see your vacation memories that didn't line up with your planned itinerary—with teenagers who refused to have their pictures made with you and toddlers who screamed during every potentially relaxing moment and everything costing more than expected.

I see you, stay-at-home mama.

I see your living room scattered with toys and your sink full of dishes and your fridge door full of magnetized summer fun ideas. I see you worried that next week you'll be standing in the driveway, staring at the back end of a school bus, wishing for another day to let your littles sleep late and wear mismatched clothes and walk around with unkempt hair.

I see you, paycheck-earning mama.

I see you with a time card punched full of work hours and void of free time. I see you longing for missed pool hours and rare snuggle time and missed opportunities. I see you gauging your summer fun on social media; I see you giving a thumbs-up and a cute red heart to things you wish you had done, places you wish you had gone. I hear what you don't say about what didn't go as planned, the places you meant to go ... you so longed to go ... you promised to go. I get it.

There just was not enough time.

The days were short, and the lists were long.

The schedule was tight, and the money was tighter.

I know you made the plans, and you intended to use the plans, and you had a heart full of good intentions that somehow collided headlong into obligations and commitments and responsibilities.

I feel your struggle.

Here's what I need you to know:
What your family wanted and needed was and is and always will be simple enough: you.

The way you laugh at their jokes and kiss their foreheads and hug their worries away—that is what makes them ready to face next week.

Whether you hugged them on a beach far away or in your kitchen right at home ...

Whether you packed up the car and traveled to an exotic destination or camped out in the backyard ...

Whether you had every day free or worked forty hours a week, no one could, or will ever be, the you who you can be.

It was all good enough and fulfilling enough and life-sustaining enough. Your people will always be your people. They will always need what only you can provide, and it will always be enough.

Let go of the expectations you think this world has of you, and recognize that no one can contribute what you can. You are uniquely capable of giving love and being loved, of fulfilling others and of being fulfilled.

Your summer was everything it needed to be.

And if not, there is always next summer.

HERE'S WHAT I NEED YOU TO KNOW
{about having a better life}

Dear kids,
     I don't want you to have a better life than I have had.
     You read that right.

It might shock you. You might need to take a seat and let that sink in. I know, as your parent, I should want better for you. *Always better.*

A better childhood, a better first car, a better education.

A better job, better technology, better relationships, better finances. Better things.

Parents are supposed to want better for their kids.

Here's what I need you to know:
I did not *have* a great childhood. I *made* a great childhood.

I played outside and made new friends. I learned not to gossip. I opened my horizons by reading. I obeyed my parents ... respected the boundaries ... accepted correction.

I did not *have* a great first car. I *worked for* a great first car.

I worked three jobs and saved my money, and I signed my name to a loan at the dealership that cost me $153.77 a month for forty-eight months of my life. I paid my own insurance and put gas in the tank.

I did not *have* a better education. I *earned* a better education.

I studied hard and earned scholarships. I spent time in the library when my friends were out having fun. I attended class and took notes and prepared for assignments and received a degree.

I do not *have* better jobs, better technology, better relationships, and better finances. I have sacrificed, worked hard, waited patiently, and earned them all.

And it's not up to *me* to see that *you* have better than I did. I don't want you to simply *have* anything.

If you want a better childhood than I had, make it.

If you want a better first car than I had, work for it.

If you want a better education than I received, earn it.

If you want a better job, better technology, better relationships, and better finances, then sacrifice, work hard, wait patiently, and earn them.

And if, by chance, you have a better life than I have had, then I will know I have taught you the value of hard work.

And that is always better.

HERE'S WHAT I NEED YOU TO KNOW
{about ruining summer break}

We have all done it.

At some point or another, we have all overplanned, underplanned, or just had no plan at all. Library every Monday? Write it down. Swimming on Tuesdays and Thursdays from 9–10:30 a.m.? Scheduled. Or maybe this will just be the summer of no plans at all. We will wing it. Schedule nothing. Be spontaneous to a fault.

I remember the disastrous summer I decided that each week we would have a new adventure. Instead, each week, I had a new headache trying to figure out how to entertain five little people now that I had promised to do so for the next ten consecutive weeks.

Big mom fail.

Here's what I need you to know:

1. **Do not think about the upcoming school year even once before August.** Listen, school lets out for a reason. Fa-get-ah-bout-it for a while. Soon enough you'll be arranging schedules and planning carpools. May sucked the life out of us all with testing and graduations and teacher appreciation and end-of-the-year crap. Let June and July have their moment to shine. August will be here demanding our full attention and our lunch account

money and our signatures on countless forms before we know it. *Don't blink. Wait it out.*

2. **Do not look at other people's vacation photos, thinking, "I wish I were there."** Here's the thing: You *aren't* there, so get over it. If you wanted to be there, you should have planned ahead, saved up, packed, and gone. And you didn't. Most of us are capable of planning a trip. We are capable of foregoing a daily coffee or newspaper or sweet tea or whatever to save for a family trip or girls' trip or solo trip. Some did and some didn't. Don't hate your neighbor or your relatives or even your enemies because they had the foresight to plan ahead. You gain nothing from that except frustration and inner turmoil. You decided early on "namaste here this summer," so stop being mad at the people who didn't.

3. **Do not make a summer academic schedule.** For the love of all things good and lovely in the world, let the kids have a break. It truly is possible for them to burn out before school even starts, and often we are the ones lighting the fire. There are a million-plus things our kids can learn over the summer that are not academic. Teach them to load and unload the dishwasher properly. Make sure they can make a bed and empty the trash and do a load of laundry from start to finish. It's actually even okay for them to spend some time mindlessly staring at the television or a screen of some sort. It's called relaxing. So relax. It's good for everyone.

4. **Do not look at "her" in a bathing suit with disgust because you don't look like her.** I realize this one is a touchy subject, but I'm just going to risk offending everyone and put this out there: Pool/beach bodies are conceived in the fall, nurtured in the winter, birthed in the spring, and adored in the summer. Ninety-nine percent of those people didn't just get blessed with good genes. They woke up, ate well, and made taking care of their bodies a priority. It's ridiculous to be upset with someone for having something you don't when they put in the work and you didn't. And wearing jealousy looks worse than an ill-fitting pair of yoga pants. It's never too late to start. So put down the bag of

chips, grab the kids, and take a walk. At the very least, you'll show the little people it's important to get moving. There's no better time than the present.

Go.

Now.

You can finish reading this later.

5. **Do not make your kids get up and go to bed on the same schedule they do during the school year.** Routine is important. There is no denying that. But one of the greatest parts of summer break is staying up a little too late and sleeping in proportionally late in the morning. Your child is not going to become an elementary/middle/high school dropout simply because they stayed up past bedtime a time or two. Everything in moderation. Let them have a sleepover or two, even if it makes you want to pluck your eyelashes out with a pair of tweezers. **They are only little once. Let them be little.**

6. **Do not insist that everyone wear matching shirts on vacation.** Before all you craft-making people pitch a fit, hear me out. I'm going to focus on the word *insist* here. If your kid/spouse/significant other desires to walk around Disney World looking like you all just walked out of a copy machine, that is just fine. Just don't force-feed them the idea. We all have that one photo of ourselves where we are wearing something someone else insisted upon. Don't let this summer be the one your family looks back on with eye-rolling regret. It actually *is* possible to have a successful family photo without everyone matching or even coordinating. Sometimes I'm just grateful all my tribe even gets in the frame. I'm going to let that be enough for me, and I highly recommend it for you also. And if everyone wants to match? Go. For. It. I'll still double tap your pictures because it will make me smile, I am sure.

7. **Do not make promises to your kids.** There are few words likely to bring about the same feeling as: "But you *promised*!" Promises are recipes for disaster. The words *I promise* are often the only words we speak that our people will remember we said,

they are almost always attached to some event we really don't want to do, and we will be reminded we said them at the absolute most inopportune time. Guaranteed. Wait? I *promised* to take you fishing today? (It will currently be pouring). I *promised* to take you shopping Friday? (It will *not* be a payday). And are you *certain* I promised to get ice cream from the ice-cream truck the *very next time* we saw one? No matter *when* or *where*? (You will have zero cash ... just like last time.) Instead of saying "I promise," just open the front door and slam your foot in it a few times ... the result is a lot less costly and painful, and your little people never even have to know.

Here's to a great summer, moms and dads. Let's make this one the best ever.

HERE'S WHAT I NEED YOU TO KNOW
{about adult children}

I folded your towels today.
    I *know* you're an adult.
    I understand this is *your* apartment and *your* space.
I know you pay bills now and buy groceries now and set your own bedtime.
    I'm aware that you are fully capable of folding towels.

Here's what I need you to know:
Folding clean towels for you is an honor.
    I am certain I haven't always known this.
    In the midst of cooking meals and hectic schedules, I didn't realize the privilege I was being given … the privilege some never get … the chance many yearn for. Being in your home, surrounded by your things and basking in the overwhelming sense that you will be okay, I wanted to find a way to honor you.
    So, I folded your towels.
    P.S. I left your socks and underwear for you. May the odds be ever in your favor, son.
    P.P.S. All your dishes are in the wrong places. That part is on purpose. Payback.

HERE'S WHAT I NEED
HUSBANDS TO KNOW
{about consignment sales}

I see it every season: Your wife, bombarding the doors, searching for the best deals.

She lines up super early.

She races through the door at breakneck speed.

She scavenges through racks and racks of clothing.

She sorts through piles and bins and tubs of toys, searching for just the right thing.

She crams her bags and stroller and wagon full of loot.

She drags a laundry basket around with a belt tied to it to use as a handle for maximum speed and agility.

She searches title after title of books and movies and games.

It's a rush, for sure.

I know *you* are home with the kids.

I know you had to navigate through school pickup and dinner duty and bedtime routine. I know she is gone for hours.

I know.

I know you're possibly hoping the kids go to bed early or don't cry or don't fight. I know you wish your wife had taken them with her. I know you worked all day, and now, when it's time to relax, real life is breathing down your neck. All so your wife can shop, right?

Sounds unfair, for sure.

I know she shops for three or four or five hours … maybe even more.

Here's what I need you to know:
She bombarded the doors because she has spent her "free time" making a list. Not a list of frivolity. A list of needs.

Who needs pajamas? Who needs a new coat? Who needs winter boots and summer sandals and ski bibs and a bathing suit? Who outgrew all their pants since the last sale? Who lost their lunch box or their winter gloves or their favorite blanket?

I'll tell you who knows.

Your wife.

She scavenges through racks and racks of clothing because she loves her kids—*your* kids—and she wants them to feel special. She loves to see them smile when they look nice. She wants them to fit in and feel accepted.

She sorts through piles and bins and tubs of toys because her children—*your* children—will have birthdays and Christmases and Easters that she will want them to remember and love and enjoy.

She crams her bags and stroller and wagon full of loot, and she drags a laundry basket around with a belt tied to it to use as a handle for maximum speed and agility, and do you know what? She gets a backache from it, and her feet hurt and her shoulders ache. But she loves her kids—*your* kids—and she wants to make the best use of her time away.

She searches title after title of books and movies and games because she knows what her children's—*your* children's—favorites are.

She knows what they mentioned while walking through Walmart. She knows what they pointed at in Target. She knows what they saw a friend wear or a commercial advertise or even more, what they just love deep down inside.

Do you know what else she knows?

She knows you are home with the kids.

She knows you're possibly hoping they go to bed early or don't cry or fight. She knows you wish she had taken them with her. She knows you worked all day, and now, when it's time to relax, real life is breathing down your neck.

All so she can shop, right?

She knows it seems unfair.

But here's what else I know:

I know she walks around using her phone as a calculator, adding up each and every item.

I know she spends hours of her shopping time sorting and resorting and prioritizing.

I know she passes by things she would love to stop and look at.

I know she only gives a quick glance at things that interest her—books by her favorite authors ... beautiful purses ... shoes in her size ... styles she loves. She skips the home-decor section altogether.

Maybe you aren't even aware that some consignment sales have those sections because she never brings those types of things home.

I know that this—this shopping—is an act of love. It is a priority because her family is a priority. Her children are a priority. And her love for you is a priority, for the hours you work and the money you earn and the time you invest in her kids—*your* kids.

I know she comes with a budget.

I know she spends lots of her time answering your phone calls about what is for dinner and when she will be home.

I also know she shows up at my checkout table stressed and concerned that she has grossly miscalculated. She watches me ring each item, and her eyes go immediately to the total when I hand her the receipt.

Do you know what else I know?

Sometimes, she literally looks afraid to even go home because she knows you will be mad that she has been gone so long or she spent too much.

It's an uncomfortable moment for us both because what I *also* know is that she's doing her best to be a good mother and a good wife, all while being a wise steward of the funds her family has.

Consider this: Maybe next time she heads out to hit up her favorite consignment sale, you could thank her and tell her that you appreciate her taking the time to do something so important for your family.

Maybe you could load the bags and the wagon that she uses while she shops into the car for her.

Maybe you could offer her some extra cash so she could pick up a purse she loves or a new outfit or something she might see to make your home look more decorative.

And maybe you could unload it all when she gets back, without any complaint about the behavior of the kids—*your* kids—or the amount she spent.

Maybe she might buy a new book, and maybe it won't mean much to you. **I can guarantee, though, it will mean everything to her.**

HERE'S WHAT I NEED YOU TO KNOW
{about cleaning}

I am sure many of you are like me. You find yourself at the end of a hard day answering the age-old question: "So, what did you do today?" If you are a stay-at-home parent, your answer is usually something like, "I cleaned. All day. That's all I did was clean up after people. For eternity I have been—and will forever be—cleaning." If you work a job outside the home, your answer is probably more like, "I went to work, and then I came home and cleaned. I am still—and will forever be—cleaning."

Often, after I have uttered these words aloud, I find myself in a sort of conundrum of conscience.

Did I *really* clean *all day?*

Have I *actually* been cleaning since I got home from my paid job?

Am I stretching the truth? Justifying? Straight-up lying?

To avoid any further confusion, I created the following list of guidelines so each and everyone of us can feel confident in our answer. Please feel free to use and/or share any and all of these with your friends.

Here's what I need you to know:
- If you spent all day doing laundry, *that's cleaning.* So what if you managed to watch an entire season of your favorite show on Netflix? You still get full credit for cleaning. You should not

be punished for multitasking. (If you emptied the dryer lint, bonus points.)

- If you opened the refrigerator to make a plan for dinner and subsequently closed it because you had to wipe peanut butter off the door handle, *that's cleaning.*
- If you took all the random crap that's lying around and put it in a laundry basket and hid it in a closet to "deal with later"—*cleaning.*
- If you piled all the pairs of shoes from around the house on the stairs for the kids to put away—*cleaning, for sure.*
- If you used a broom to sweep the carpet in your bedroom because you left the vacuum upstairs like a month ago, *that's cleaning.* This also falls under the category of exercise, so bonus points. Take yourself out for ice cream later.
- If you sat down to create a list/spreadsheet outlining the cleaning chores for the day/week—*cleaning.*
- If you ran your finger across the top of the television because you weren't sure the last time you dusted it, *that, my friends, is cleaning.*
- If you filled a sink full of hot, soapy water to "soak" the dishes, that's *totally cleaning.* If you remembered to dump the cold water out and fill it with hot water again before dinner, bonus points again.
- If you dramatically threw clothes to the floor of the closet because they didn't fit, *that's cleaning.* If you actually placed them in a bag to get rid of "later"—*cleaning.* If you flailed around in anger at how you've "let yourself go," bonus points again for exercise.
- If you reached into the tub to pull out the large ball of hair covering the drain and then grabbed the closest towel nearby to wipe the edges of the tub clean so you could take a "relaxing bath," *that's all cleaning.* Not even up for debate.
- If you lit a candle to cover up the lingering odors of kids and pets, *that's cleaning.*
- If you read an article about how to streamline your cleaning, give yourself credit. That's research, and it still counts.

- If you took a trip to Dollar Tree or Ikea for some containers to organize things in and then came home and put the bag on the floor and promptly forgot about it, *it still counts as cleaning.*

- If you looked under the kitchen sink to verify that you are, in fact, out of glass cleaner and then took time to notice that you were also out of bleach, dishwasher detergent, and disinfectant, that's all cleaning related; therefore, *it's cleaning.*

- If you moved everything around in the pantry hoping to locate one single pack of Kool-Aid so the kids would stop complaining about there being "nothing to drink," *that's cleaning.* It's also organizing, so good work!

- If you restarted the dryer so the clothes could "fluff up," *count that as cleaning.* No one in the family deserves wrinkled clothes.

- If you rifled through the drawer/cabinet/basket of plastic containers trying to locate a lid for the leftovers from dinner and managed to match a few other lids with their partner containers, *count it.* That job is basically one step away from the entrance to hell itself and deserves to be recognized as such.

- If you scraped dried cereal off your comforter so you could sit down and rest a second (because, duh, you've been cleaning all day), *that's cleaning.*

- If you shoved all the random crap from inside your car quickly into the trunk because you forgot it was your day to take the entire volleyball team home after practice—*still cleaning.*

- If you wiped an unknown gummy substance off the screen of your computer/tablet/phone so you could log in to social media, *that's cleaning.*

- If you opened the "junk drawer" and, while looking for one AA battery, managed to take out and throw away all the old, dead batteries that your family for some reason decided to save, *that's highly detailed cleaning,* and it counts majorly. Reward yourself with a break.

- If you sprayed cleaner into the toilet so it could "soak a bit," that counts. Even if you forgot to go back later and actually scrub the toilet, *give yourself cleaning credit.* Your intentions were good.

I am sure there are many more we could all add to the list. Feel free to add them. **Take it easy on yourselves, mamas.** This world would be a dirty place without you.

HERE'S WHAT I NEED YOU TO KNOW
{about becoming a mother}

I saw you today at the pool, mother to be.

I saw your gloriously large, bulging-with-life belly.

I saw your adorable messy bun or topknot or whatever it's called these days.

I saw your neatly packed pool bag, complete with snacks and a good book and all things sunscreen.

I saw your sun-kissed cheeks and your tanned arms.

I saw your fluffy, like-new beach towel … I am sure it smelled of fresh detergent.

I saw your classy, scratch-proof, polarized sunglasses.

Many years ago, I was you.

I was just on the verge of motherhood. I was eager with anticipation.

I was ready to meet my little one and show them the world.

I had hopes and dreams and nervous excitement and fear.

I was sure my child would be valedictorian and also sure that they would never learn to breastfeed correctly.

I was convinced I would raise a child who would become a doctor or a lawyer, and I was also just as sure that they might end up a homeless beggar.

I was certain I would have a child who loved God and maybe would become a preacher just like their father, and I was also maybe just as sure they might become a serial killer.

I thought it all.

I compared my belly to those of other pregnant mothers.

I compared my skin tone to that of others.

If I knew my neighbor read to the baby in *her* belly every night, *even on the weekends,* I wondered if I should be reading to the baby in my belly more.

Did I need a gate or a fence or even a wall to protect my little person from getting out into the world? Did I need the same to keep the world from getting in?

I wondered if my house was equipped enough to raise a child and if my heart was big enough to love one.

Would I be able to stay home?

Would I be able to work?

Could I honestly say I was ready to commit my life to following another human being around for at least a minimum of the next seven to ten years *every minute of every day,* minus, possibly, some time while they slept?

Would I ever read another book or go out on another date or take time for myself at the gym?

Would I ever even sleep again?

Would I forget my child in the tub or the church or the store or—God forbid—the car?

Was I even capable of mothering?

Here's what I need you to know:

You will do it all wrong, and you will simultaneously do it all right.

You will have moments of sheer genius, and they will be preceded or followed just as quickly by moments of sheer madness.

Sweet mama, your hopes and dreams and excitement and fear are all valid, and they are all okay.

If your child is valedictorian, that will be amazing.

If they never learn to breastfeed properly, guess what? That is okay as well.

If you raise a child who becomes a doctor or a lawyer, fantastic … but homeless beggars have mamas too. They have people who love them and miss them and pray for them and want to hold them and that is all okay. You might raise a child who loves God. Cling to that. Verbalize that. Embrace and proclaim that. They might become a preacher. That would be incredible. But serial killers have mamas as well. And it's not the mamas' fault. They still love their children and miss them and pray for them and want to hold them.

Keep your focus, mama.

Don't look to the neighbor on the right or the neighbor on the left for your validation.

Don't watch another woman walk the aisles of the grocery store and wonder how you measure up.

You were only meant to be you, and your sweet child was meant for the parents they are born or adopted into, and every bit of that is in the master plan.

You will laugh, and you will cry, and you will curse, and you will pray.

You will watch your dreams rise and fall, and you will watch their dreams do the same.

And one day, one day that will be here much sooner than you could ever believe possible, you will be me.

You will see the fresh mamas just starting this journey and you will remember it all.

It's all worth it.

Let your journey be your own, and allow your mama friends to have their own journeys as well.

If so, everyone will have much more to talk about sitting on the park bench in a few years.

HERE'S WHAT I NEED YOU TO KNOW
{about comparison}

I see you.

   I see your weary eyes and tear-stained cheeks.

   I see your well-dressed littles and know deep inside you have neglected yourself for their sake.

I hear your trembling voice.

I watch your insecure mannerisms.

I feel your comparison. Your gauge. Your determination to "measure up."

I get it.

I see you.

I hear you.

I feel you.

I am *you*.

We are raising these humans, and we are trying to keep our sanity.

We have walked away from careers and hobbies and spontaneity, all for the sake of twenty-plus years from now.

We aim for meaningful conversation, but we end up with small talk and awkward silence.

We plan purposeful events and memory-building moments, and we end up with blurry pictures and blurry eyes.

We try to capture it all, and in the process, we miss so much.

We are seeking to be all things to all our people, and we keep losing track of ourselves.

We won't give ourselves a break or let ourselves off the hook.

This thing … this motherhood thing …

It's so hard.

It's painful to our bodies and our hearts and our core.

And so we isolate ourselves in a cocoon of safety and routine.

We stick to the plan, and we clean up the messes, and we look around at the end of the day and wonder how we will do it all again tomorrow.

And some days, if we are being brutally honest, we don't want to.

We want to sail away into the sunset … drive away and not look back … pack a bag, grab a map, and go searching for the person we lost along the way.

Our people—they *need* us.

They need us for dental appointments and haircuts and toilet paper and school pictures.

They need us for concert attendance and lunch money and white poster board at ten at night.

They need us for forgotten papers and winter coats and food … *all the time, food.*

Here's what I need you to know:
They need us for so much more than that.

They need us for validation and for inspiration and for recommendation.

They need *hard truth*.

And *fierce hugs*.

And *honesty*.

They need us to be okay with ourselves, with our bodies and our minds and our choices.

They need to know that we can love them because we love ourselves and we love each other.

We can't go around clipping each other off at the knees because we have a better recipe or a better house or a better life.

We need to be a tribe.

We need to have each other's backs when we fail. We need to reach out and help each other up and be for each other what we need most for ourselves. We are a team, mamas.

If we raise our kids to think we have all the answers and we need no one, we raise them to believe a lie.

If we raise them comparing and complaining, we will reap entitled, selfish adults.

If we don't let them see we are vulnerable and that we fail and that we need each other, we raise them to believe they can exist alone ... and they will become bitter, lonely adults.

Look around, mamas.

Phone a friend.

Make eye contact.

Look across the parking lot or grocery store aisle or waiting room office.

We are there.

Each and every one of us. We need each other.

Every. Single. Day.

Don't give up. Hang on. **Be the help while you wait for the help. Meet the need while you are needy. Reach out a hand when you feel most like reaching into yourself.**

Together, we can make this thing happen.

And even if we never have a Pioneer Woman meal or a Joanna Gaines home or a Jillian Michaels body, we will have each other.

There is strength in numbers.

Look for me because I will be looking for you, sweet mama friends.

We've got this.

HERE'S WHAT I NEED YOU TO KNOW
{about field trips}

There is a running dialogue that is held at our house a minimum of twice a month. It usually goes something like this:

Unnamed Student: Mom, did you remember I need a bag lunch for my field trip.

Me: When is the field trip?

Unnamed Student: Ummm ... I don't know. Maybe tomorrow.

Me: What do you mean, you don't know? How am I supposed to remember when you have a field trip if *you* don't even remember you have a field trip?

Unnamed Student: Mom. Why are you yelling?

Me: I am not yelling. I *can* yell, though, if you'd like to know what yelling sounds like.

Unnamed Student: Gosh, Mom. I just need to know if you remember I need a bag lunch. It's not that big of a deal.

Me: How is it not a big deal? Do you want to be the only kid on the field trip, *whenever it even is*, without a lunch? Do you want to be *that* kid? Do you want all your friends and your teachers to think we cannot afford food? Or that you aren't loved?

Unnamed Student: I think you're acting crazy now. Maybe you even *are* crazy. I just need a lunch ... for whenever the field trip is.

Me: HOW AM I SUPPOSED TO PACK A BAG LUNCH WHEN I HAVE NO IDEA WHEN THE FIELD TRIP EVEN IS?

Unnamed Student: Now you most definitely *are* yelling.

Me: OH YEAH, KID! YOU HAD BETTER BELIEVE I AM YELLING NOW! I NEED TO PACK A LUNCH FOR A FIELD TRIP THAT YOU HAVE NO IDEA WHEN YOU ARE LEAVING FOR, AND SOMEHOW I AM SUPPOSED TO REMEMBER SO THAT I CAN MAKE SURE YOU HAVE A LUNCH LIKE ALL YOUR FRIENDS WHO HAVE MOMS WHO ACTUALLY PAY ATTENTION AND KNOW WHEN THEIR CHILDREN WILL BE LEAVING THE SCHOOL CAMPUS!

Unnamed Student: Mom, seriously. It's like you are losing your mind. You signed a form. It had all the information on it about the field trip. And I'm pretty sure it's tomorrow.

Me [*basically on the verge of a full-on aneurysm*]: WHAT DO YOU MEAN I SIGNED THE FORM? WHAT FORM? DO YOU MEAN ONE OF THE SIXTY-FOUR THOUSAND FORMS YOU BROUGHT HOME THE FIRST WEEK OF SCHOOL THAT HAD TO BE FILLED IN WITH BLUE OR BLACK INK ONLY, NOTARIZED BY A NONFAMILY MEMBER, AND THEN COPIED IN TRIPLICATE AND RETURNED IN THE MANILLA ENVELOPE THAT I AM SURE I MAILED COUPONS TO YOUR GRANDMOTHER IN? IS THAT WHAT YOU MEAN? THOSE FORMS? THE FORMS THAT ALWAYS HAVE ALL THE PERTINENT INFORMATION, LIKE WHEN THE BLESSED FIELD TRIP EVEN IS, ON ONE SIDE AND THE PART WHERE I SIGN MY NAME ON THE OTHER, THEREFORE GUARANTEEING THAT WHEN YOU TURN IT IN, I IMMEDIATELY LOSE ALL OF THE INFORMATION I WOULD NEED TO AVOID THIS CONVERSATION? IS THAT THE FORM YOU MEAN?

Unnamed Student: Ummm ... I have no idea what the right answer is. I think those are the forms I'm talking about.

Me [*trying to get it together so the neighbors don't call the police*]: Listen, I just need to know when the field trip is so that I can make sure you have a lunch. Is that too much to ask? Surely at least *one* teacher today would have mentioned if the field trip to which you are referring is tomorrow, right? Surely, they don't just expect that it was mentioned *one, singular* time and that you all would remember? I feel pretty sure that if I were to march into the school right this very minute, the date of the field trip would be written in dry erase marker in *every single* classroom you visit *every single* day of the school year. Is that what you want me to do? March into the school right now?

Unnamed Student: Mom, it's like nine o'clock at night. The school is closed. And locked.

Me [*trying out some yoga/meditation breathing I accessed via a YouTube video one time*]: So just to make sure I am understanding you: You need a lunch. A bag lunch. For a field trip. You are not sure when the field trip is, but I signed a form giving you permission to go, so somehow, I must know when you need the bag lunch. Is that about right?

Unnamed Student: I feel pretty sure this is a trick question. Is Dad around? Maybe I could ask him.

Me: Please. Feel free to ask your father. I am sure he will know. And please feel free to let him know all about this trip you are going on. Where are you even going?

Unnamed Student: I have no idea where we are going. If I knew that, I might remember when we are going.

Me: There is no logic in your statement. I do not think I even gave birth to you. Anyone I gave birth to would be sure to remember when they would be boarding a bus to leave the actual school campus to go to wherever you are all going. Anyone with my genes would know when the trip is and where the bus is going.

Unnamed Student: Ooooh yuck, Mom. I don't need your jeans. Just a bag lunch. Maybe it's on the website.

Me: Oh yes, *paaahhlease* let me access the website. That's always fun. Let me search around hither and yon for the username and password that I can never remember. Let me see if I can navigate through all the notifications about the Girls Only meeting and the book fair and the sports schedules for the week, and somewhere BURIED IN THERE LIKE A TREASURE JUST WAITING TO BE FOUND will be the information I seek. I'm sure that will be exactly how that goes.

Unnamed Student: I think I'll just pack a lunch tomorrow just in case. And would you happen to have some spending money? I think we may need some, for wherever we are going.

Here's what I need you to know:
Y'all think I'm kidding, I am sure. But I assure you this happens.

Every. Single. Time.

Teachers, can you help a mother out here? Can you please just make sure those dang forms with all the pertinent information are printed so that I can keep all that info at home? I know that when I need to cut that bottom portion off, I will grumble and complain that I can't find the scissors, but that's a problem for another day.

Please and thank you.

HERE'S WHAT I NEED YOU TO KNOW
{about fancy things}

Y'all …

Last week, I ate dinner at a *fancy* restaurant.

Now listen—here is the part where I leave out the name of the actual *fancy-to-me* restaurant, lest there be some naysayer out in cyberland who feels the need to say something as unhelpful to the universe as: "Actually, I wouldn't consider [insert name of unmentioned restaurant here] to be a fancy restaurant."

For the love of baby Moses floating in the sweetgrass basket, there were *no* paper napkins, there was *no* plasticware, and I saw *not one* solitary child the entire time I was there.

That, all summed up, equals fancy to me.

After searching the actual parking lot fruitlessly for a spot, I found a gravel side lot about two continents away. I left my car there covered in anointing oil, said a prayer that it would be there when I got back, and marched my way across the gravel/asphalt/concrete parking area in my wedges (because what is a possibly fancy dinner without wedges?).

I stopped partially through my journey to take a picture of the building. (Because after all, if I eat a meal at a fancy restaurant and don't post a picture, did the meal actually even happen? Ummm, no, Mark Zuckerberg, it did not.) And I made my way to the front doors.

Upon entering the doors, I found myself face-to-face—literally because it was stainless steel—with an elevator.

Score: Fancy 1, Not Fancy 0

There was a sign next to the elevator that said something about the rooftop being closed due to a private party.

Clearly, I was not headed up there.

Y'all, as Jesus of Nazareth is my witness, I stood there a full four minutes staring at the doors of that elevator. I didn't push the button. I didn't look left or right. I literally just stood there, paralyzed, staring at the doors as if I were considering jumping off a high-rise building or something. One would think I had never ridden an elevator before in my entire forty-something years of life.

At some point in my nearly catatonic state, the doors of the elevator opened for me, and I was confronted with some restaurant patrons and a young girl dressed all in black holding menus. I used my deductive reasoning and concluded she was an employee, so I asked her which way I needed to go to the main dining floor (never mind the fact that none of them exited the elevator, which left me wondering where in the world they had just come from).

After a cute little snicker, the hostess assured me the main dining floor was up, and we began our ascent, at which time she said, "We are headed to the fourth floor."

Now, it made total sense to me that by "we" she meant she and her patron friends, so I just figured we were riding to the top *first* before finding the floor I was supposed to exit on. (And, because my actual entrance into the restaurant was taking so long, I was pretty sure my friends were well past appetizers, so what was a little joyride at this point anyway?) So I just stood there as the doors to the elevator opened on the fourth floor as promised.

And no one moved.

Not the patrons.

Not the cute young employee in black holding menus.

And not me either.

I just stood there, waiting for the doors to close so I could go back down to the floor I was supposed to get off on.

Finally, after a long, awkward pause, I said, "Oh, is this the main dining room floor?"

The cute, young waitress said, "Well, yes," as if I was supposed to be a clairvoyant or something.

Sheesh.

Here's what I need you to know:
A little direction goes a long way.

The rest of the evening was amazing and uneventful, in a good way.

The food was all unpronounceable to me and fancier than our finest meals at a family gathering. The sangria was fruity and fresh, the conversation was light, and my dish was rich and hearty.

I decided I like fancy restaurants. I guess I'm going to need the hubby to get a part-time job.

Or maybe I could just get a job riding up and down that elevator, directing people to the correct floor. I feel certain I could be a little more helpful.

HERE'S WHAT I NEED YOU TO KNOW
{about unconditional love}

I held you when you took your first breath.

I fed you and clothed you and showed your beauty off to anyone who would look.

I saw your first smile.

I heard your first words.

I memorized your laugh.

I watched you learn to crawl, then walk, and eventually run.

I witnessed you learning to read and write.

I watched you grow strong and happy and healthy.

I watched you suffer illness and pain and heartache.

I have had a VIP pass and a front row seat to your whole life thus far.

I have been your manager, your boss, your coach, and your cheerleader.

I have raised you to be strong and independent, and yet you have always allowed me the blessing of holding you up when you have been weak.

I have loved you with my whole heart, and you have loved me back. I have felt it.

You have been my best friend and my strongest supporter.

You have been my confidant and my biggest fan.

I would know your laugh, your voice, and the sound your feet make coming down the stairs apart from anyone else's.

I have loved you from your conception.

I have always told you I would be here for you no matter what.

I have always been and always will be right by your side in a moment's notice.

I have prepared you to embrace adulthood and live a big, full life. And now, we are literally days from packing you up to start that life.

But now, before you leave, there are a few other things I need you to know:

Do you know that I have needed you as much as you have needed me? That when you took your first breath, I inhaled differently … almost as if for the first time?

Do you know that when I fed you and clothed you, my soul was fed and my heart was wrapped in a blanket of love and contentment?

Do you know that now, all these years later, your smile fills my heart just as much as it did the first time I saw it?

Do you know that the sound of your voice—even when it's frustrated or harsh or angry—still makes me well up with all kinds of feelings?

Do you know how happy I am that I have memorized the sound of your laugh? Do you know how often I replay that sound in my mind when I am apart from you because it is one of the most beautiful sounds I have ever heard?

Do you know that when I watched you crawl and then walk, I was always filled with so much pride at your progress? Your pace was ever quickening and your feet slowly began to move with stability and assurance. Do you know that now, before you leave, all I can think about is how much I wish I could slow you down?

I need you to know that my love has always been and always will be unconditional.

I will be here when you are strong and happy and healthy.

I will hold you when you suffer illness and pain and heartache.

I will always buy the VIP pass for the front row seat to your life, and although I may no longer totally be your manager or your boss, I will always be your coach and your cheerleader.

You will never be even one mile too far away from my love.

You will never call at the wrong time or need me when it is inconvenient. You will never be alone. I will always be here. Maybe a little more in the background but still always here.

Be brave.

Be confident.

Have fun.

Be smart.

Never settle for mediocrity.

Never allow someone's disrespect or dislike for you to change the person you are.

Not everyone will love you, and that's okay.

Be you.

Don't imitate or copy others. You were born unique.

Be that.

I love you far beyond any of these words.

Our worlds are about to change, but my love for you is constant.

Dream.

Love.

Live.

Go.

You have my blessing for it all.

I love you forever and beyond.

HERE'S WHAT I NEED YOU TO KNOW
{about August}

It's August.

It's the last couple weeks of summer, and *this* mama is feeling it.

We have bought enough glue for slime recipes to keep Pandora's box locked up tight forever. My kids may never even know the actual real purpose for glue. Ever.

We have replaced a certain leaky bicycle tire tube not once, but twice.

We have hidden painted rocks ... and found painted rocks ... rehidden painted rocks and found even *more* painted rocks. Yes, rocks. Those things filling the driveway that we have been kicking out of the way for years. They are cool now, it seems.

We have all watched more TV than can possibly be safe for the psyche. Like seriously—who can watch TV like that? All. Day. Long? My people can—that's who.

The littles have created a YouTube channel where they make stuff and open stuff and do stuff. Mostly make slime, I think. Go figure. Yes, I am aware it's not safe for kids to be on the internet. No, I really don't even care anymore—it's August.

The three middle schoolers have spent 97.4 percent of the summer arguing with each other. Pick a topic. They are not particular.

"THAT'S MY SHIRT!"

"WHY DID YOU TAKE THE COMPUTER? I WAS IN THE MIDDLE OF AN EPISODE!"

"WHO ATE ALL THE CEREAL?"

"WHY ARE YOU SPITTING ON ME?"

The list is endless.

I am fairly certain that just last night I uttered the words: "I am so tired of hearing their voices. I need my own house." Yes … I said those words out loud (but out of earshot, so that's better, right?).

We attempted to be *that* family. We made a trip to the library and got the summer reading chart and checked out books. We then returned them late, one with severe water damage from a dip in the pool. I seriously could've bought all the books we checked out for cheaper than all the fines I owe. Their reading charts never got completed. I know you are shocked.

Last week, the girls started looking for their summer work packets. You know, the ones they send home crammed in the kids' book bags at the end of the year along with every art project they ever did, twelve tons of loose paperwork, and all the stuff you've been missing from home all school year. ("So that's where all the scissors went.") The packets they worked diligently on the first week school was out and then misplaced for the rest of the summer. The packets that are supposed to be turned in when school starts back in just a few weeks. Yeah, those packets.

School is just around the proverbial corner. The stores have had school supplies out for weeks and every time I walk past them, I feel like a terrible mother for not buying my kids sticky notes in every color and erasers shaped like hot dogs.

This summer has been extremely hot. I have said, "Close the front door!" 3,455,765 times. I stopped saying please in mid-June.

My people have consumed a gallon of tea a day and two gallons of milk a week, used every dish in the house twice a day, left crumbs and food particles on the counters after every trip through the kitchen, and *still* they can't remember to see if the dishwasher is accepting dirty dishes before just plunking down their plates wherever. Just feel free to leave them anywhere in the house you like, small people I birthed. I don't mind walking around the house like a busboy, all day every day, stopping science experiments from growing in your cups and bowls. I have lowered the bar of expectation so far, you can now step over it. And with school starting in literally days, my most predominant thought is this:

I miss them already.

In just a few short weeks, we will all get back to a schedule. There will be no more sleeping until noon or eating cereal at two in the afternoon just because.

We will be back to early mornings and homework and sports practices and PTO nights and so much other *stuff*.

The eldest boy will be starting his senior year of college, and I will be forced to resort to video calling with my eldest princess, who somehow will have convinced someone she is old enough for college! Like zombies, the littles will pass me in the kitchen and mumble something about signed forms and lunch money and ask, "Have you seen my [fill in the blank]?"

And another year will pass, and they will grow older and be home less often and begin to stare at phone screens rather than look into my eyes.

Here's what I need you to know:
These days don't come back, mamas.

Celebrate the last of summer.

Take the too late trip to McDonald's for ice cream.

Watch too much TV and eat too many sweets and peek around the corner and watch your kids play.

Too soon, it'll be routines again.

Let's fill these last days with enough memories to get us all through at least winter break.

Then we can start planning ways to hide from them again.

HERE'S WHAT I NEED YOU TO KNOW
{about healing}

I recently had an emergency appendectomy.

It obviously wasn't how I had planned to spend that Wednesday night, and coupled with the fact that it happened literally the night before my beautiful daughter's graduation from high school, the timing was not opportune. But my body decided to send an eviction notice to my appendix, effective immediately.

Surgery was fine.

Recovery in the hospital was fine.

Getting home and settled and taking meds and resting was fine.

Ten days later, I was fine.

And yet, I wasn't.

I was still moving slowly. I hadn't been cleared to exercise or lift anything. I tired easily, I felt disoriented at times, and I just didn't feel like myself. And sometimes, even on a really good day, my wounds were sore to the touch. They looked good, and they were healing nicely, but they ached and reminded me of what happened.

I told my mom about how I felt and she said—so simply— "Remember ... your body is healing from the inside also."

So simple, yet so profound.

This was a fact that I hadn't really considered.

I knew my scars were mending, and so I felt like I was going to be back to my always-on-the-move-never-slowing-down me. I was disappointed that I wasn't able to do all I normally did or act like I normally acted, even though, from the outside, everything seemed to be just fine.

Here's what I need you to know:
There is so much of life that seems to work in this seemingly reverse process where things look just fine and appear to be healed on the surface. And yet when someone presses just right, we ache and are reminded that we've been wounded.

And that's okay.

There are times in our lives when we choose poorly, and our decisions hurt us.

And sometimes, things just happen ... things beyond our control and out of our hands, and then our hearts hurt and our wounds gap.

Sometimes, we heal so well on the outside. And sometimes, someone comes along and their words press deeply into our wounded places.

Sometimes, even on a really good day, our wounds are sore to the touch. They look good, and they are healing nicely, but the ache is there, boomeranging us back to the moment of injury.

And all that is okay.

The hurt keeps us humble, and the tenderness reminds us of our humanity.

Sometimes the ache is a glaring reminder of what hurt us, and sometimes it is a gentle nudge, reminding us of what we survived.

We all have hurts, and we all have wounds, and we all recover from the injuries of life at our own pace.

Sometimes we move slowly. Sometimes it hurts to lift anything, and shame from others is the hardest burden to lift. Sometimes we tire easily and feel disoriented, and we just don't feel like ourselves.

And wouldn't it be amazing, if, in the midst of all our pain, we just gave each other a little grace? If we just said to our people, "I see the pain. I know you are healing, and I know you are tender ... but look how far you've come." Could it even be possible to smile and hug someone who's hurting and look for ways to help them?

Wouldn't it be life changing if we just looked past the superficial surface and heard the hearts of our people? If we allowed humanity to be, well, human? If we stopped setting expectations and guidelines and time constraints on life's injuries, and we just listened closely … and closed our mouths … and opened our arms wide … and took in the injured and recovering, the damaged and bruised, with only love and patience and empathy?

And what if we could do it all without ever inserting our opinions?

Wouldn't we all heal better this way?

Maybe it wouldn't hurt to touch our own wounds every now and then as a reminder of the power of the human body and spirit and, even more importantly, as a reminder that we all heal better when we are touched gently and with grace.

HERE'S WHAT I NEED YOU TO KNOW
{about future you}

I don't think I actually saw you until around day five or six. Shamefully, that's the honest truth ...

Even though our husbands had been swimming and fishing together some part of each day, and even though I was sure you were around somewhere, I just didn't see you until it was the day before you went home.

It's possibly because I had my face stuck in a book. (Yes, I had time to read a book!)

You looked beautiful. I am sure you will disagree, but you did. You wore your motherhood like a fine gown. Your swimsuit was stylish, and your cute baseball cap made you look like you belonged on a magazine cover. I am sure you struggled with even finding time to get dressed for the beach, and I am sure the hat was probably more for lack of time to style your hair than for sun protection, but you looked adorable ... seriously!

I already knew you had littles. I had seen your boy playing with my kiddos in the water day after day, chasing the waves and asking his daddy tons of questions about fishing as he bobbed up and down in the pulsing ocean. I am sure it was unnerving everytime his head went under the water as you waited for him to resurface.

I didn't see your sweet little girl until that same day I became aware of you. I loved watching you chase after her and keep her occupied in a place that held lots of potential danger.

I loved your zest and your zeal and your sunglasses ... Yes, I *really* loved your sunglasses. (Mine are prescription, and they are old and too expensive to replace. So I really was taken in by your cute sunglasses.)

You looked so *together*. Your parents were there, and you told me y'all were making Beaufort Stew that night for dinner. It sounded yummy, and I secretly thought about following your sweet family back to your rental house to sneak some for myself.

We talked about the dangers of swimming in the ocean and kids growing up and how tiring being a mother to small humans is.

We talked about sunburns and where we each lived and how much you needed and were enjoying this vacation. You said how much you longed to actually sit at the beach and read like me. (I was literally standing in the ocean having this conversation with you while my book was still in my hand.)

I remember telling you how tired it made me just watching you care for your little people and how I knew that I must be getting old because watching them run around made me tired. You chased after them and kept from danger in the waves and made sure they had adequate sun protection ... and food ... and drink ... and entertainment ...

And I had time to read a book.

You commented ever so sweetly how you couldn't wait until the time when you could finally read a book on the beach, and I chuckled and said something about it being here before you knew it. And when you left our conversation, you packed up the astronomical amount of stuff it takes to bring a family with littles to the beach—the tent and the cooler and the toys and the kiddos—and you gracefully herded everyone to the cute little golf cart you rode back to the rental house.

And I had time to read a book.

Here's what I need you to know:
While it looked like I was reading, sweet girl, let me tell you what was actually happening.

I was sitting in my beach chair—I am sure looking quite relaxed and subdued—wishing I had remembered to bring the bathing suit top I had actually purchased for the beach ... the one I wasn't 100 percent sold on but bought anyway just so I wouldn't wear the same one I had worn for the last several years. I was wondering how smashed up my hair was going to be from being under that hat all day ... that hat I was wearing because, even though I had time to fix my hair, I just wanted to get to the beach to watch my kids play.

I was also watching my tribe play in the water, asking their daddy tons of questions about fishing and bobbing up and down in the pulsing ocean. It was unnerving every time their heads went under the water as I waited for them to resurface.

I was thinking how I wished I had your zest and your zeal and your sunglasses ... Yes, I loved your sunglasses *that* much.

I was slowly turning pages and thinking about the dangers of swimming in the ocean and about my kids growing up and about how tiring being a mother to teenagers and adolescents is.

I was constantly rereading the same sentences and thinking about sunburn and how much I needed and was enjoying this vacation. I was also thinking about how grateful I was to be able to sit in a chair by the lapping waves but a part of me was jealous that you had littles to chase and build castles with.

I was also wondering if my kids had adequate sun protection ... and food ... and drink ... and entertainment ...

Yes, I had time to read a book, but I did very little reading.

We never stop mothering.

We never stop worrying and wishing and dreaming and wanting the best for our kids.

The grass always looks a little greener somewhere else, sweet friend. But it's only our vantage point that changes.

Embrace these moments.

They won't last forever, and they will be in the rearview mirror of that cute golf cart before you blink.

You are investing wisely and wonderfully in the future of our world, and even when you doubt your self-worth or your abilities or even your swimsuit and hat, you are doing well, my friend.

Keep on getting after motherhood. Every day is a choice between living and existing. I watched you *live* at the beach, and I am a better person for it.

You reminded me of the brevity of childhood and the importance of being present in each and every moment.

You reminded me of me—ages ago and today also. I remember second-guessing every decision and wondering if I was doing it "right."

You are enough, young mother.

Your contributions are enough, and your value is enough, and the only yardstick with which to measure yourself should be the one your Creator alone made for you with the wood from the cross he hung on.

The days will pass, and the tables will turn, and *you* will be sitting in the chair watching littles play and envying the sunglasses of a stranger.

All while some young mother thinks you are reading a book.

I hope someone shares this with you. I sadly don't recall your name. But I will remember your face and your hat—and yes, your sunglasses— forever.

HERE'S WHAT I NEED YOU TO KNOW
{about regret}

I'm sorry.

I don't really know where else to begin.

I'm sorry that I didn't take the time to notice what an obviously terrible day you were having before I asked if you wanted to switch seats.

Thank you for saying "yes."

I'm sorry that whatever dreams and plans you had didn't work out and that you found yourself moving back home, broke, and "in so much trouble"—your words—and I'm sorry that it obviously broke your heart and made you feel like a failure.

I'm so sorry that when you placed a video call to your mother, you didn't hear the words you wanted. I don't know your history with her. I don't know any part of the story, so it would be unfair for me to take a side with either of you. I do know that your mother probably loves you more than you'll ever know ... even if the words she said—yes, the words we all could hear—didn't convey that message to you.

You heard her words; I heard her heart.

I'm equally sorry that when you called several friends, you had to quickly relay the story of how the person who was supposed to purchase your plane ticket for you didn't and how that left you alone at the airport. I'm sorry you ended up having to call a ride-share service to the tune of sixty dollars because you had no other way to get home.

I'm sorry you had to put out six hundred dollars for your one-way ticket back to your new/old life.

Here's what I need you to know:
I wish I had been brave enough to strike up a conversation. **I wish you and I had made eye contact so maybe then I could have found some words of comfort for you.**

I'm sorry that this world has let you down. I'm sorry that all you could do was be sad, lean up against the window, cry, and sleep.

Can I just be honest?

I was flying home from an amazing trip. I was with my daughter, and we had just enjoyed an incredible six days together, hanging out and making new friends. Selfishly, I didn't want to have to take my thoughts off what I had just enjoyed … not even for a stranger possibly in need.

I'm so very sorry for that.

I'm mostly sorry for this: When I heard you say, "Why does God hate me?" on the phone, I didn't interrupt you and assure you that God could never hate you, that his love for you is so big and so far-reaching and so complete that there's nothing you could ever do to change that. I'm so sorry that you possibly left that plane believing God didn't love you.

I have prayed for you since then. I have asked God to forgive my selfishness and to wrap his arms around your heart, heal your wounds, and provide the things you desire and need in your life.

And I believe he will.

And I'm sorry if my decision to not engage you in conversation made things worse. I hope, should you ever read this, that you will find it in your heart to forgive me.

HERE'S WHAT I NEED YOU TO KNOW
{about the book fair}

'Twas the day of the book fair, when all through the house
not a creature was stirring, including my spouse.
The flyer was hung on the fridge with such care,
announcing the dates all the books would be there.
The children were clinging to pillows and sheets,
in rooms that I swear at some point had been neat.
And I, in a T-shirt and old baseball cap,
decided to wake all the kids from their naps.
When out from the kitchen there arose such commotion,
I hurled dirty laundry in one sweeping motion.
Away to the kitchen I flew like a flash,
dropping laundry and dishes my children had stashed.
The light from the fridge, flashing Water Below,
gave that pale, yellow flyer a near-neon glow.
When what to my sleep-deprived eyes did appear,
but a tiny fifth-grader, her face filled with fear.
With her sweet little hand so lively and quick,
I knew in a moment what was making her tick.
More rapid than eagles the announcement it came,
as she whistled and shouted and began to proclaim:
"We have to get ready! We have to leave now!

We cannot delay, we must get there somehow!
The book fair is there!"—her words shot like a bomb—
"And it's not just the book fair, it's Muffins for Mom!"
"YOU HAVE TO BE KIDDING! HOW COULD I FORGET?
THE FLYER HAS BEEN UP FOR A WEEK OR MORE, YET …"
As mail had been scattered and read and replied,
somehow this event had almost sneaked by!
So out to the car with their book bags they flew,
while I emptied the change jar (what else could I do?).
And then, in a twinkling, I made up my face,
threw some clothes on my body, put my hair back in place.
I glanced at the flyer, it's mocking quite loud,
and I knew there was no way to beat the big crowd.
I drove to the school, had to park in the grass
(because that's where you park when you're basically last).
We raced in the door, made our way down the hall,
got our muffins and juice and our napkins and all.
I finally got brave and took a quick glance,
to see if others were as late, by chance.
What I saw made me laugh, no more fear, no more shame.
I could tell all the other parents felt just the same.
It was like *Walking Dead* had just met LuLaRoe;
the teachers moved quickly, the parents moved slow.

Here's what I need you to know, in case anyone listens:
Could we maybe skip muffins and have other fixin's?
And maybe instead of a Monday so early,
we could do Friday night, say at like, 7:30?
And instead of that juice and those sweet, savory things,
could we have some mixed drinks and some hot chicken wings?
Overall, I am glad for the time with my littles;
they are growing so fast, and I know the time whittles.
Thanks to all those who planned and who served and who care,
from a mom who was rushed, but was glad she was there!

HERE'S WHAT I NEED YOU TO KNOW
{about Valentine's Day cards}

I saw you in Dollar Tree and again in Walmart.

I saw you hastily making your way through and around the holiday aisle, eyeballing what was left of the boxed Valentine's Day cards.

The choices were seriously meager, what with it literally being the day before the big event. It's become such a "thing," this celebration of February the fourteenth.

I was there also, with my cart holding some ingredients to finish dinner for my family and a few random gifts for friends of the littles.

At first, you didn't see me looking …

I saw you glance at my cart and shamefully look down at your hands that held several boxes of store-bought Valentine's Day cards—the kind kids have given out at Valentine's Day parties for ages. The kind my mom and probably your mom bought for us long before Pinterest was even a thing.

Then you caught me looking at you …

Our brief eye contact said volumes: you were in a hurry; dinner would be late; yes, an entire year had passed since last Valentine's Day, but somehow you still managed to procrastinate and wait until the proverbial bell was tolling to get Valentines; you didn't have a lot of money to spend; and you were tired … so very, very tired.

We both went on about our business, you looking sheepish for being caught with the easy-way-out Valentines, me looking down in shame because I had been caught looking at you.

I assume you, like me, tried to find the shortest line that you could in order to check out in a hurry and race home to get done all that the evening held, including slapping some names on those boxed Valentine's Day cards you had just picked up.

That was technically our last interaction.

But sweet mama with the store-bought Valentine's Day cards, here's what I need you to know:
I saw you again when I got home. In myself.

You see I, too, used those store-bought Valentines for my kids this year. And after purchasing those few remaining ingredients to finish dinner for my family that night (which also included the fresh fruit and chocolate chips I was supposed to have already sent in for the classroom mom to set up for the party)—the ones that I should have gotten hours ago—I was racing home to watch my kids slap some names on those same Valentines and shove them in a grocery bag to take to the party the next day.

I, too, was in a hurry.

Our dinner also would be late.

Yes, I also had been provided an entire year since last Valentine's Day, and somehow, I had still managed to procrastinate and wait until that same proverbial bell was tolling to have my kids finish their cards.

I, too, didn't have a lot to spend.

And I, too, was tired ... so very, very tired.

You and I are probably very different in many ways. But I suspect we also are alike in many ways. I have felt the similar sting upon seeing the amazing creations friends and friends of friends had come up with. I mean, I never knew there were so many ways to convey the same message.

I have gone to the party and wondered who had time to make cards with an actual photo of their child on them ... one for every single child in the class? Who had time to research, design, shop for, and create these masterpieces? Did their days somehow have more hours than mine? Were they more creative? More efficient? More generous?

Did they love their kids more?

Was the detail in the design of the cards the barometer of love for children? Was the level of love for your child measured by the quality of the Valentine's Day cards they handed?

I have felt all these things, and I have asked myself those questions countless times. And I have always come to the same conclusion: *no.*

Those handcrafted, beautiful, trendy Valentines don't make anyone *more* or anyone *less.* They make us different.

Some of us have the time, some of us make the time, and some of us just aren't interested in how amazing our Valentine's Day cards are.

Some of us love crafting, some of us have time to craft, and some of us wouldn't build anything unless we were stranded on a deserted island and needed a shelter desperately.

Some of us are old, some of us are young, some of us have one child, and some of us have many. And all those things make each of us unique—not better or worse—just unique. The way God intended us to be.

So mama with the store-bought Valentine's Day cards, hear this message loud and clear:

You are enough. Your effort is enough. Your heart is big enough, you are doing enough, and your store-bought Valentine's Day cards are enough.

I love the people who post pictures of their amazing Pinterest-inspired designs. Some of the best people I know are those people. Their hearts are big, their ideas are amazing, and their schedules are different from mine. **But I have learned that judging the quality of my motherhood by comparing myself to other people never results in me feeling better about myself.**

Someone will always have more time.

More money.

More creativity.

Better Valentines.

And that's totally okay with me because I am *me*, and sweet mama, you are *you*. Be you.

You are enough.

HERE'S WHAT I NEED YOU TO KNOW
{about the ends}

I made French toast for the kids this morning.

Today's Sunday, so me actually cooking anything is rare. Feel free to judge.

We also skipped church. I'll leave the reasons why that is okay for another piece at another time. Just trust me on this one: God isn't taking attendance, and while the fellowship and routine and spiritual growth from attending church is great for us, it's not always what gets us pulled up close enough to the throne to whisper our concerns into the ears of an ever-faithful God.

I could offer a range of real-life reasons why we skipped: The hubby worked overtime all weekend and left again this morning with the sunrise to work another full day. We spent four-plus hours at the ER yesterday evening with our eldest daughter, having her checked out for a possible concussion after she was rear-ended on her way to her second job of the day. (No concussion, thank God.) We got the call about that accident literally just after parking the car at the outlets where my husband and I were going to finally knock out some of our Christmas shopping. (The littles keep ever-so-politely saying how they can't wait to see presents under the pretty tree. I know this is their way of saying, "There *will* be presents, right?") I also had to leave from our eventful night at the ER to pick up one of the littles at a friend's house at

11:30 p.m. because they went to see Christmas lights, but she doesn't spend the night away.

I worked all week. He worked all week. You get the point.

Back to the French toast.

I scrambled up some eggs, added some milk and cinnamon, and made beautiful pieces of lightly toasted bread. Made-for-TV French toast. Food Network-worthy.

Well, maybe I'm exaggerating a little, but the point is that it looked beautiful on the plate, the kids ate as much as they wanted, and all was right with the world.

Until I finally got around to making my own.

And, of course, there were two pieces of bread left—my two least favorite pieces—the ends. Now some people out there love the ends of the bread. Me, not so much. And I'm not going to lie—I felt a little frustrated that, once again, my kids got the best, and I got the leftovers.

Then, right there in my little kitchen that was all decorated for Christmas, I thought of how I used to watch my mom make meals for us time after time. And time after time, I watched her serve herself last and eat what was left ... often, I am sure, the ends of the bread.

Raising little people is a sacrifice in so many ways that many people will never understand.

Whether you grow tiny people inside your own belly, you adopt them, or you help raise the village around you, it's all parenting.

And it's all hard.

We live in a society that makes us feel all our moments need to be Instagram-worthy. We need to filter it all, take out the imperfections, and try to fool everyone into believing we have it all together. We look at the snapshots of other people's days, and we immediately feel like we don't measure up.

A friend recently texted me (a guy friend, oddly enough) and asked me how I kept my house clean when my kids were little.

I thought about telling him about the "eleven minutes a day" house-cleaning plan I saw online. I did actually tell him a few suggestions I had that would make life a little easier. But then I told him the one piece of advice I wish I had heard as a young parent: let it go.

There will be time to clean later. Keep your house sanitary and picked up, but don't stress if it doesn't look like a magazine photo.

Stop comparing your real-life movie reel to everyone else's perfectly staged snapshots. That is not reality, and we all know it.

What I know is this:

My husband is hard at work, out of town for the day at his second job, traveling many miles to make those Christmas presents a reality for our tribe. He works five days a week at one job and at least one really long day on the weekends at another to make life happen for our people.

My eldest son will be home any day from completing the first half of his junior year at college. He is healthy and makes my heart swell with pride every time I see him. He is struggling through some hard things right now. He is growing as a man, so I sleep with the phone on the bedside table and with the ringer turned up to full volume so I will always be accessible.

My eldest daughter is sore, but alive, after what could have been an awful tragedy. She has been in two accidents in the last three weeks that were not her fault and could have resulted in very different circumstances. I am giving her ibuprofen and heading to Walmart for a heating pad, not planning for her funeral. I do not say that for dramatic effect. I say that because it is truth.

My middle boy told me the French toast was "amazing," and he could taste the cinnamon (see why he wants to be a chef?). He watched all four *Home Alone* movies yesterday because he was, in fact, home alone. He could have chosen a much worse way to spend his day.

I have one twin soaking in the tub because she has a huge (and I mean *huge*) tangle underneath her beautiful head of hair that yours truly will get the pleasure of untangling soon. I am not looking forward to that task.

And my littlest little woke me up with texts this morning from her friend's house to see what I was doing (sleeping) and what my plans were for the day.

My life could be better, I suppose. I don't really choose to see it that way. What I choose to see is that my family is loved and happy and healthy. We do not have all the worldly possessions that make us look like a success in the eyes of many. Our house is small (and when I say small, I mean all seven of us share about eighteen hundred square feet or so when the college boy moves home from campus). We only recently got rid of an eyesore of a vehicle and replaced it with a car I love. We have to all work really hard to make the ends stretch close enough to meet week after week. Our house is crowded, and often I find myself praying no one randomly stops by because it's cold right now, and stepping outside to talk to them might not be polite.

But we are thankful and grateful.

Mothers and fathers, keep on pressing through. Sisters and brothers and aunts and uncles or grandparents raising grandkids or dads or moms doing life alone … don't give up. Friends doing more than your fair share of carpool duty and teachers having to be more like moms and dads than teachers—don't quit.

Here's what I need you to know:
We are the ends of the bread.

We are what holds the whole thing together and keeps all the little inside pieces from scattering away. We are firm and rigid and steady. Yes, we are steady.

There is no middle without the ends.

This thing we call life is often held together by such a flimsy grip. We mess it up, and we want to quit. But we are the ends. We are what keeps the middle soft and fresh and pliable. Our steady hand is what allows our people to lose their grip sometimes because they know we will hold them together and that we are on their side.

Don't give up.

The years will pass quickly, and at some point in time the house will be clean, and the laundry hamper will be empty, and the fridge will be full. (I have been told these things by others.)

We only have so many years. Let's make them count. Ends and all.

HERE'S WHAT I NEED YOU TO KNOW
{about what I would change}

Dear kids,
Some days, it seems like I have been a mother forever. And then some days, like today, it seems we just started this journey.

You five have changed my world in a million ways. I wouldn't change a thing about being your mother.

There are, however, so many things I wish I could change for you all—too many to list for sure.

Here's what I need you to know:
I wish you didn't have to eat. Like every day.

Seriously.

It would be so great if I could just do a Meal of the Week and y'all would be satisfied. I am sure the quality of the meal would increase significantly from what you all get now. I might even actually open one of the twenty-three cookbooks I own. You can thank yourselves for my poor culinary skills.

I wish you didn't have to learn to drive.

Ever.

That driver's ed teacher who has to brave the open road once, maybe twice with y'all behind the wheel gets to ride down Easy Street. I, however, get multiple chances to face death head-on ... times five. Only three of you drive without an adult present as of yet, and I'm already sure I have prayed for sweet Jesus to take me home at least a dozen times.

Also, I wish you didn't need an education.

Yes, I wrote that.

I wish I didn't have to drag your catatonic bodies out of bed each and every sunrise and force-feed you breakfast like it's diet food at fat camp.

Every one of you knows you can hear me calling your name five mornings a week. Why y'all try to act like one morning I'm just going to give up and let y'all sleep in is beyond me. School should start when you are old enough to drive yourselves—which brings me back to the previous point. Case closed.

And stop acting like I overnighted new book bags from L. L. Bean in the middle of the night and that you don't recognize yours when it's time to go to the car.

Just. Stop. It.

I wish you only had four changes of clothes, like we pack for vacation. I will never understand how you can create so many varying outfits out of the limited clothing you pack for a trip, and yet, when home—where you have unlimited options—you still wear the same things over and over. It's enough to make me want to stick my own head in the washer and set it on the spin cycle.

And shoes. Don't even get me started on those.

We could open our own shoe store, and y'all would never even miss the ones we sold.

Next, I wish I could go to the Dollar Store without you.

Every. Time.

It never ends up being a bargain for me. I go in for plastic sandwich baggies and two birthday cards and somehow end up with an ashtray shaped like an elephant ("Mom, [fill-in-the-blank] *loves* elephants") and yet another pencil pouch ("Mom, the last one broke").

Want to know why it broke? Because it came from the Dollar Store! It's starting value was nine cents, brand new.

And *no*, we do *not* need any more sidewalk chalk, twenty-four-piece puzzles, or candles that smell like summer! I have smelled summer. These candles do NOT smell like summer!

And how can you possibly need a poster board for yet *another* school project?

Every. Single. Week.

Who even does real projects anyway? Isn't everything digital now? Didn't they finally outlaw the science fair?

Furthermore, I do *not* want to buy Christmas ornaments that you just L.O.V.E. in September! It still feels like the devil's backyard outside so, *no*, I do not want to purchase items containing fake snow that you will not be able to locate next week, much less in December!

I wish you had to do one entire school year without the internet—or any technology.

I wish you had to build a time line out of a toy construction set and pick up an actual newspaper, scissors, and glue to do a current events project.

Your lives would change. I guarantee it.

I enjoy raising you all ... *most days*.

HERE'S WHAT I NEED YOU TO KNOW
{about Monday}

It's Monday, y'all.

And can I just say it has already felt like it in so many ways?

This morning, as I backed out of the driveway with the two littlest littles on the first of three trips to three different schools, one of them (no I don't remember which one … it was early, people!) pointed out a roll of paper towels in the driveway. It was a brand-new roll still wrapped up in plastic.

I knew it had fallen out of the truck, but we were in a hurry, so I told them I'd grab it when I got home to pick up middle child for trip number two.

Only the adorable seven-month-old puppy found it first.

Yeah, it's Monday …

My goal all morning was to clean the house. It needs it and I'm home. (And let's face it, no one else is volunteering.) It is only 9:40 a.m., and I have already done three loads of laundry (with, I am sure, at least three more still to go). I swept and steam mopped the kitchen and dining room. I gathered trash and picked up stuff.

So. Much. Stuff.

Socks and shoes and toys and leftover craft supplies and dishes and dishes and more dishes.

I have moved and sorted and washed and wiped, and I still have so much to do. How in the world can these people I share this space with make such a mess?

But my perspective is different today.

Last night my biggest boy was robbed while making a pizza delivery for work.

Robbed.

He made the delivery, and when walking back to his car, someone came up behind him, knocked into him, and demanded his money. He handed it over without question, and the person ran off. I am grateful for bosses who care enough to have trained him to give the money without question. (And that nothing is worth his life.)

I remember getting a call from a friend of his who said he had been robbed and that she couldn't get a hold of him. My head began to do that swivel thing that happens when your world is tilted slightly differently on its axis, and you can't get your bearings quite right. So I called, his phone went straight to voicemail, and I tracked it. It seemed to be moving, so I kept calling and kept getting his voicemail. I texted and kept calling. I called his work and got his boss, who said he was back (inhale) and was okay (exhale) ... shaken up, but okay.

Safe.

This mama slept very little last night.

Here's what I need you to know:
This mama is tired. I have gone over and over the situation in my mind, and I can't imagine that it really happened. I see in my head all the ways it could've been such a different story ... with such a different outcome. How today I could be visiting a hospital—or God forbid, a funeral home. How my entire world could have been upended in a single moment. How nothing would ever be normal again. How that moment could have forever divided our lives into "before" and "after." How I could be trying to remember last words or last moments.

How drastically different this morning could have gone.

And how that laundry could still be waiting for me to get home to do it.

So as I sweep and mop and pick up and wash and wipe, I am purposefully mindful of how blessed I am that today holds only housework.

Every piece of dirty clothing is a reminder of the six other blessings who live here.

Every dirty dish means there were people here to feed.

Every piece of miscellaneous "stuff" means that life is normal ... and good ... and okay. **This house is lived in, and it looks lived in—but we are all *living*.**

Today could have been so much different.

I'll take the mundane tasks and consider them a gift today, a gift I am truly grateful to God for. I know he guarded that boy of mine. I have no doubt.

Every one of our stories and substories could potentially end differently than the reality. Sometimes things don't turn out like we expect and that's okay; we learn to accept what we cannot change and adapt to it. But sometimes things end way better than they could have.

And for those times, we should be extra grateful.

HERE'S WHAT I NEED YOU TO KNOW
{about laundry}

Dear son,

I know you have a very hectic schedule, and seeing how today is already Tuesday—your laundry day—I thought I would help you out this morning by getting your laundry started. I realize that you had so much to do this morning, what with waking up and getting dressed and all. I know that tying your shoes and choosing a T-shirt can really slow a morning down to a screeching halt, so I wanted to take the pressure off you and give you one less thing to stress out over today. I know that it weighs heavily on your mind each Tuesday, and that last night was eventful since you had to actually locate the charger for your iPhone and plug in your school-issued tablet.

I'm just here to help make life a little easier for you. It's a goal I strive for daily, and I hope I am doing a job that meets your satisfaction.

Now, back to your laundry.

I have some concerns. I honestly am quite worried about you, and I'll tell you why. And then I'll tell you what I've done to help you out.

First of all, I noticed that most of the clothes are near the hamper but not actually in the hamper. This makes me very concerned about your vision. I measured the hamper, and it is eighteen inches wide by twenty-four inches long—much larger of an opening than, say, a typical basketball goal. I know this because in doing my research while trying to figure out how to help you, I looked it up online and found out that a typical goal is eighteen inches in diameter.

See? Much smaller than the hamper opening.

This is what has led me to worry about your vision. Maybe it's a depth perception problem. Maybe those new glasses you have had for a month or so (the glasses that have already been broken and are now at the repair shop) aren't the right prescription. Maybe the problem is minor and can be taken care of by a simple visit back to the eye doctor.

Regardless of the issue, I know that basketball season is rapidly approaching, so I took the liberty of contacting the coach at your school to let him know you wouldn't be trying out. I want him to understand that your health is much more important to me than basketball, and I don't want you trying out, not being able to see and aim, and then being embarrassed when you miss the shots and subsequently don't make the team. Like I said, I'm here to help you out in any way that I can.

Consider that problem solved.

You're welcome.

Next, I am very concerned about your stamina and strength. I realized as I lifted the hamper out of the spot it stays in that it was very light, due to the limited number of items actually inside it. That caused me to look around at the surrounding floor, and I was astonished to realize that you must honestly have zero energy. I mean, the floor was littered with clothing near the hamper (which I now realize is a vision problem). I also now see that you must not even possess the little bit of strength it would require to bend over and pick the items up and place them into the hamper right next to them. This scares me. It could be a sign of so many things.

I called the doctor, but getting an appointment for such a serious case may take a while, so I also took the liberty of calling the head football coach. There is no way he should expect you to be able to do things like up downs and push-ups, and I certainly wouldn't want you to have to run and get tackled. I mean, with your vision problems already being what they are and with the total lack of energy added to that, it's just a recipe for disaster. A trip to the ER in the making.

So now that you don't have football practice to worry about anymore, you should be able to work on getting adequate rest, and that should help you rebuild your energy.

Again, I am only here to help you.

And again, you're welcome.

Also, regarding your strength—I took the liberty of contacting the school cafeteria manager. I know how much you like to pack a lunch from home, but I realize now that taking snacks and such must be contributing to your overall poor health, so I asked her to make sure you ate only cafeteria food from now on. I know what time and attention the government puts into making sure that the meal is nutritious and meets all the food pyramid requirements. At home, I basically just throw some stuff together (usually leftovers from family dinner the night before) and land it in the lunch bag. Your health should not have to pay the price for my lack of enthusiasm in the lunch-packing department. Therefore, you can now count on five days a week of a healthy, nutritious, school-issued and monitored lunch—complete with a pint of milk! No thanks needed.

Lastly, I know that overuse of your eyes can cause eye strain, so I have removed the television from your room, disconnected your cell phone, and set your tablet for school use only. I know that watching TV at night is a habit, so I thought taking the television out would help make it easier to break. Also, that screen time on your phone involves using fine motor skills, and since your gross motor skills are so poor, I have now removed the temptation to stare at a screen for hours as you further harm your already limited eyesight. You will thank me later.

Here's what I need you to know:
I love you, son.

It is my privilege to be your mother, and it's a job I take very seriously. I hope the things I have done for you today will have you on your way to recovery quickly and that we will look back and laugh one day about how you used to not be able to make a few items of clothing land in the hamper with such a large opening. It will be a funny story for a long time, I am sure. No thanks needed. Seeing the look on your face when you find out all I have done will be satisfaction enough.

Trust me.

Love, Mom

HERE'S WHAT I NEED YOU TO KNOW
{about quality time}

I got a call recently from my eldest.

Isn't that sweet? He's in college and busy with school and work and studies, and yet he takes time out of his busy day to just shoot the breeze with his mother.

Yeah ... I didn't buy it either.

Can we just be real here? If a college junior calls his mom and starts the conversation with "So what are your plans tomorrow?" you can count on one of four things:

1. He needs food.
2. He needs money.
3. He has dirty laundry and is in danger of having to go to class naked.
4. Any combination of the above.

As overjoyed as I was to see his number pop up on my cell phone, I also knew this probably was going to cost me. I like to live in reality, people.

This time, it was laundry.

I do not feel obligated. He is, for heaven's sake, an adult. But I know my times with him are short, and I want to cherish each chance I get to see him. So if doing his laundry means I get a face-to-face conversation, even if it's only when I pick up the looming pile of dirty stuff and when I drop off the sweet-smelling, neatly folded pile, then so be it.

I'm shameless when it comes to my boy.

This time, though, he used a word he had never used before. He caught me off guard. He asked if I would *help* him do his laundry. As in *we* would do it *together*. Like a team. Meaning not me alone.

I jumped at this offer like a woman with a stuffed purse sitting in the audience of *Let's Make a Deal*. Watch out, Wayne Brady. This deal was mine.

So we met up and dragged his seemingly endless pile of stuff into what has now become my regular laundromat. (I parked in my regular space, which actually isn't even a real parking space, and he stared at me like I had two heads. I like the spot, and I'm claiming it as mine.)

It took a little time to make a plan, but we finally concluded we would need two washers that my entire family could physically fit inside and then another smaller one that would hold his brother's laundry that I had brought with me. (Hey ... I was already going be trapped there, so I might as well bring some of my own work from home.) If I had any doubt as to whether he had done *any* laundry at all since the semester started, I now had my answer: nope.

He began helping me load clothes into the washers, and I suggested he turn them all right side out so he didn't have to do that when they were wet or before folding. He complied, and then he moved all the socks and underwear to the side. Perplexed, I watched a bit and realized he was figuring out which socks went together so he could wash them together. In actual pairs. Like they originally came from the store.

Be still my beating heart.

The laundromat process is long, and the scenery is less than stellar, but we watched and waited.

We laughed and stared at a pair of underwear that got trapped in the door of the washer and was being twisted and turned over and over again and then untwisted and unturned over and over again. He told me it was his favorite pair, which made me laugh even more. It was about time something that was *his* favorite suffered unfortunately in the washer. We finally made enough progress to get it all loaded in dryers.

(We decided on five so that things could have some room to flip around and theoretically would dry faster.)

And then it was finally time to fold.

I am an expert at folding. I have folded enough clothes to qualify me for some kind of medal, I am sure. He, on the other hand? I wasn't even sure he knew how. Yet there I stood in amazement at how capable he was. He folded (and he folded well, I might add). And what's even more? He asked the sweet, underpaid employee there if he could buy some hangers so he could hang, yes *hang*, his favorite shirts.

And he paired socks and folded some more.

And then, as I was placing something in one of his baskets that I had folded, he so very politely asked me to put it into the other basket, the one with more of the same type of clothing. He was actually categorizing his stuff into groups.

All joking aside, I got a lump in my throat. An actual lump.

Here's what I need you to know:

I have messed up so many things in my life. So many times I have failed to come even close to the mom mark that has been set, whether real or perceived.

I have hurt people I love, and I have let down those who held me up the highest.

I have walked a very broken path, and sometimes I have just lay down in the middle of it, wishing it would all just end or go away.

I have missed being the best mom by a long shot, and I am sure like many other women out there (or at least those of us real enough to stop "Fakebooking" our lives away), I have failed a million times or more.

And yet, God gives me continued blessings.

Sometimes they are in the form of jobs to work to earn some money, and sometimes they are in the people he has blessed my life with who are willing to look past what I have done and instead look at who I am.

And sometimes, it means witnessing a child do something that confirms inside that at some point, I did something right.

This boy is amazing, and I am his mother.

No matter what I have failed at, I have succeeded in raising amazing children. I don't take all the credit for that. They have an amazing father, and we serve a loving, forgiving God.

But I will take a little credit because I know the enemy wants me not to. He wants me to miss days like today by being caught up in all that went wrong. (Today alone we lost the transmission in one car, and as I was typing this my daughter called, saying she was stranded on the side of the road after *her* car had died. Daddy to the rescue. Not to mention I totally forgot a promise I made to another child and broke her heart. Yeah, I failed *big* today.)

But I refuse, at least for today, to be sidelined by where I failed; instead, I choose to be lifted up by the areas in which I have been successful.

Our needs are often great, and it is easy to focus only on the ones we feel are not being currently met.

But I am going to claim the small victories when I can. Watching my son fold laundry, I know I have succeeded in some areas. And that menacing little voice from you-know-where that doesn't want me to acknowledge the wins? Today, I told him where to go.

There are many days when the struggles seem to outweigh the successes, and it feels like I just keep looking up, only to still be under the surface of the water.

For today, however, I am going to reflect on that time my son thought we were only doing laundry.

HERE'S WHAT I NEED YOU TO KNOW
{about the night before school starts}

I t's the night before school starts and all through the town,
lots of children are grumbling, from high school on down.
The lunches are packed with those gluten-free meals,
and the backpacks are stuffed with those great Walmart deals!
The teachers are ready; each room has a theme.
The posters are hung, many sporting a meme.
The pencils are sharpened; the desks are in place,
making sure that each student has adequate space.
The buses are gassed up; the routes have been set.
Pick-up tags are on dashboards; carpool families have met.
Olympic sports are recording, bedtimes drastically dropped,
and no more late-night walks to check out PokéStops.
The clothes have been picked out; new shoes have been bought.
Tax-free weekend was hectic, but such great deals we got!
Vacations are over; late-night swims are no more.
Porch lights go off so soon on those monogrammed doors.
Nighttime falls fast as kids get in their beds,
fluffing pillows to rest under freshly washed heads.
Lights have been turned out; bedtime prayers are all said,
everyone giving thanks for their fresh, daily bread.

But sometimes the stories are far, far from that,
and the families look different, bank accounts not so fat.
Some children will not have the things that they love;
many kids will be lacking things mentioned above.
Their backpacks are threadbare, their clothes not so new.
They may not have gotten new socks and new shoes.
Supply lists were used as a guideline instead
so that parents could buy things like milk and like bread.
Their families are fractured, their lives much the same.
They often have siblings with different last names.
And none of this makes them bad people, you see.
It's just that they're different from you or from me.

Here's what I need you to know on the last night before school
starts back up again:
As we tuck in our children, let's please remind them.
That being a friend is of no cost at all,
and we all deserve love so that no one feels small.
Being kind is important; being the same is not.
It's about who we are, not about what we've got.
If we teach our kids that, all else falls into place.
Love is for every person, religion, and race.
Love your friends, hold them close, but don't ever lose sight;
the things you have now could be gone on this night.
And remember the ones who have less than we do
because people are people, like me and like you.

HERE'S WHAT I NEED YOU TO KNOW
{about sandwiches}

It happened again … this time, while we were on vacation.

You all were contentedly playing in the ocean; I was reading a book. It was as hot as Satan's back porch out there that day. Everyone was occupied, and then someone said the dreaded words, "I'm hungry. May I have a sandwich?" That's all it took for you all to gather around like vultures—waiting—as I started getting all the things I would need out of the picnic basket.

I made sure it was all near me so I could assemble each one of you a sandwich quickly and efficiently, and yes, I will admit, I was stalling for time.

I could feel all your beady little eyes boring through me. I knew you all were waiting to see if that would be the day I finally remembered. I laid out slices of bread and fumbled around with the mayonnaise and mustard for an excruciatingly lengthy amount of time.

I kept waiting for someone to crack … for a sweet little voice from some gene carrier of mine to speak up and say something—*anything*—but nope.

You stonewalled me; that's what you all did. Stared me down while sweat dripped down my back. You all knew what you were doing.

So here it is.

I will finally admit to what we all (within the walls of our family) have known for years:

I do not remember what condiments any of you take on your sandwiches.

There.

I spelled it out for you.

I have tried to hide that fact. I have tried to pretend it was all a game and that I *really* knew but wanted you to think I didn't.

I have made up mnemonic devices to try and trick my brain into remembering. All for naught.

I just can't do it.

Someone likes mayonnaise.

Someone *hates* mayonnaise—not just doesn't like it but literally *gags* over it.

Someone likes mustard *only*.

Someone wants mustard *and* mayonnaise.

Two people like the same thing. Who those two people are, I don't know. I wish I did.

And then there is the ham versus turkey and the lunch meats versus the good ole classic PB and J … grape versus strawberry … white bread versus wheat …. It's like a flashback to every math word problem I have ever done, all rolled into one huge dilemma.

The list seems endless.

And I don't have even a clue anymore who wants what.

Here's what I need you to know:

I don't really care that I don't know.

That's right. I am tired of all the sandwich shaming in this family.

All the "Good moms would know" and "I can't believe after all these years" and my personal favorite "Really?? Again? You *still* can't remember?"

Enough is enough.

I don't know, and that's that.

I have good reasons not to know. I have a head full of stuff to remember!

Do you all realize how much information is already in my head? I learned all the needed material to graduate from both high school *and* college. I have memorized social security numbers and driver's license numbers ... And now I have to remember when the last time you went to the dentist was because that tells me the last time you had your teeth cleaned, therefore letting me know the last time you had a new toothbrush.

I remember to schedule your eye doctor appointments and which of you now wear glasses.

I have to remember to register you for school. Every. Single. Year.

I remember to wash your favorite blankets you like to sleep with and to hang uniform shirts in a place they can be found and which softballs are the game balls because they don't get thrown in with all the other random sports equipment.

I know what size shoes each of you wears and who is allergic to amoxicillin and who hates thunderstorms.

I remember to wake you for school each day and to make sure your report cards are signed and that you have a solid-colored short-sleeved shirt for the chorus performance (elementary school folks) and black pants that fit and black shoes that were seemingly impossible to find and buy (middle school son).

I know where your vaccination cards are, where the tax records for our family for the last zillion years are, and where the tape and scissors for wrapping presents are kept (inside the mint green basket on the top, right-hand side of the bookshelf in our room, just in case you wanted to know).

I know what's in the freezer and how long ago the plants were watered.

I know the last time each of you showered. (Some of you don't even have to tell me—it's fairly obvious.)

I know that all seems like extraneous information compared to knowing what you take on your sandwich.

I also have other things to remember.

I am busy spending my days soaking in the sound of each of your voices. The thought of someday forgetting that is overwhelming.

I want to remember how it feels when you reach out to take my hand while we are shopping or how you feel when we snuggle while watching TV.

I have reserved space in my head for memorizing each and every inch of your faces ... and the look when our eyes meet.

I am grasping tightly to the time that is slipping away while I try to face that at some point you will stop calling me Mommy, you will stop needing my supervision, and you will possibly stop wanting me to be so involved in your lives.

I want to always save room for the amazing conversations we have had.

I know what the looks on your faces mean (which is also how I know y'all were stalling, waiting for me to confess that I didn't know what you wanted on your sandwiches).

I have etched your first words, first steps, and first heartbreaks into my mommy brain. Every time I forget something, I fear that I will forget everything.

Every. Single. Time.

And that fear causes me to work overtime to bring to the forefront of my mind all the things I never want to forget ... *ever*.

I never want to forget that amazing feeling when I first held each of you. I never want to forget the first time you voluntarily took my hand.

I never want to forget to say, "I love you" and "I miss you" and "I'm sorry."

I am so scared of forgetting what really matters that I am not ashamed of not knowing what you want on your sandwich.

My goal all along has been to raise amazing children who love God, serve their families, work hard, and for the love of all things holy, can make a sandwich.

So if you are hurt that I can't remember what you take on your sandwich, suck it up.

Or even better, make your own.

HERE'S WHAT I NEED YOU TO KNOW
{about reality}

I t isn't supposed to be like this ...
    I am *not* supposed to be down on my hands and knees scouring the bedroom floor for the remote control ... again.

I mean, honestly, there are only two people who actually live in this room ... TWO.

I understand there are five other people who seem to *think* this is their space, but it's not. So the remote should be—theoretically—right where I left it when I cleaned up the bedroom this morning.

Right on top of the tall, green dresser.

Right in front of the television itself so that when it is needed, it is easily found. Please tell me that—at least in theory—I am right.

Of course, in *actuality*, what is in front of the television on top of the tall, green dresser is a small pile of mismatched socks.

I will admit I placed the nomadic socks there of my own accord. I found them while folding a load of my eldest's laundry. (Yes, he is home from college, and yes, this means he has graced the floor of my laundry room with his overflowing stash of clothing, begging one to wonder why anyone should ever need so many T-shirts and athletic shorts.)

I had the small pile of socks in my hand to take to the (I am ashamed to admit) much larger pile that sits in a basket in the laundry room waiting for me to force some child to match twenty pairs before being able to go wherever it is they want to go. I was on my way to the laundry room to put the socks in their proper location. Honestly, I was.

They were *in my hand*, but I put them down when I noticed the loose change and trash on the dresser. I couldn't just ignore trash and money, so I sat the socks down to pick up the trash (which I placed into the kitchen trash can) and grab the loose change (which I added to my not-so-secret coin can in the kitchen cabinet).

It was then that I noticed the kitchen looked as if a small tornado had blown through. So I unloaded the clean dishes from the dishwasher and loaded it up again with the dirty ones.

This then led my eyes to settle on the countertops that needed to be wiped down. *Really*? Is no one who lives here capable of seeing this mess?

Obviously, I needed a clean rag to wipe with, so I opened the cabinet beneath the sink only to discover that there were, indeed, no clean kitchen rags available.

Sigh.

Why, any sane person would wonder, would there be no clean kitchen rags? Not even one?

I'll tell you why ...

It's because they were all piled in the sink on top of each other where apparently the little people who live in this house put them after wiping up multiple spills ... each with a different rag, of course. That is what led me to grab the pile of dripping wet, sticky rags and take them to the laundry room. *Oh, the laundry room*. The room my eldest has decided is his video game playing domain whilst he is home for the summer. The room that always somewhat resembles a cross between a bachelor pad and a homeless shelter.

And, is it even possible to *start* a load of laundry without having to first *unload* a pile from the washer, open the dryer to discover that there is a load waiting to be unloaded, take the dry clothes out and find a place to set them, *reload* the dryer, and then pick up the load you took out of the dryer so you can carry it to the bedroom to be folded? Or is that just in my house?

Here's what I need you to know:
It's due to the need to fold the clothes that now grace my bedspread that I find myself looking for the television remote.

Which is obviously not where I would have left it.

Which is why I am now searching the floor near the edge of the bed.

I found it—just in case you're curious.

And I rejoiced quietly, plopping down on the bed to fold the clothes at my feet, aiming the remote at the television to turn it on.

Which did nothing, due to the small pile of mismatched socks … directly in front of the sensor.

HERE'S WHAT I NEED YOU TO KNOW
{about the last five dollars}

I did something today that I don't usually do: I picked my own kids up from school.

Go ahead—let the judging eye rolls begin. Lean over and whisper to whomever you are near while reading this something like, "Can you believe she doesn't pick her own kids up from school? I mean, she doesn't even work a *real* job." And then take another sip of your latte and scroll through your social media on the most up-to-date technology while your kids play in their afternoon play group specifically designed to improve their gross motor skills as well as expand their interpersonal relationships.

I could waste your time and mine and list the myriad of reasons why I usually can't get there as the bell tolls. But I'm fairly certain what would sound like great, logical reasons to me would sound like excuses to most everyone else, so we will skip the part where I list, and you can just pretend to agree.

Some parents excel at the whole after-school, mother-of-the-year pickup thing. I used to do afternoon dismissal duty as a teacher and assistant, so I know what these moms look like.

They always manage to clear their schedules of all other duties, allowing them to roll up to the car rider line at least forty-seven minutes before their darlings will even be dismissed. They come prepared with the latest, best-selling novel, ready for consumption. They have healthy, nutritious snacks—kept at the appropriate temperature for the season of the year—ready to hand to their precious cargo the second they drop their angelic bodies into the car. No trash falls out when they open the doors, and it always smells like sunshine and a cool ocean breeze inside their cars. Their hair is always neat. Their stylish sunglasses are perched daintily on their heads, no matter the season (after all, the sun is always shining at some point during the day, right?). They always have their car tag displaying their child's name in easily read print, making it very easy for the lady with the walkie-talkie to call their child out. They have a seasonally appropriate beverage for their own consumption, probably in an environmentally friendly reusable cup. They have on shoes. And bras. They stop their cars, roll down the windows, and commune with nature while they wait for the end of the educational day for their little Einsteins.

Then, there are the rest of us.

We are usually headed to school, already behind schedule, when we realize the gas light has mysteriously come on ("Didn't I *just* fill up yesterday?"). We skid into the gas station, pump three dollars worth of gas, forget to put the cap back on the tank, and race out, leaving the pump still displaying the "Would you like a receipt?" message. We arrive just in time to race up to no colored cone or number in particular because honestly, at this point, there isn't even a line anymore. We have no car tag, but it's irrelevant since only three kids are left standing there. The eternally patient teacher assigned the afternoon car line duty opens the door for our little blessings, at which time we *pray* the empty foam cups/trash wrappers/dirty clothes don't fall out, creating a proverbial yellow brick road for our children to walk upon to get into the car. We mouth something unintelligible about "traffic" or "lost keys," and we race away before anyone has time to ask if we signed up to bring a baked good to Parents' Night. (Wait? There's a Parents' Night?)

So you can see why I was proud of my accomplishment today. I had no *real* work today, after all. I leisurely did a speed clean of my kitchen right after *restarting* the washer that I found with the lid still open when

I went back to transfer the laundry to the dryer. I grabbed a teenager's forgotten lunch—I honestly placed it *right* by the front door! How could she *possibly* have missed it?—and hurriedly ran it into the school office, where I basically threw it at the sweet, smiling secretary. I then raced over to the high school to drop a book off for a friend. When I finally managed to get back home, I gathered all the trash and loaded it into the back of the truck, ran a Mother's Day card to the post office (yes, I *know* Mother's Day was yesterday!), made a deposit at the bank, grabbed enough groceries to make dinner, and then, realizing I had eaten no food, used all but five dollars of the cash I had in my possession to grab a quick bite at Subway.

This is the point at which I realized it was now time to pick up my two precious jewels from school.

I am pretty sure I was the last car in line. I am also *quite* sure I could read both the teachers' and my little darlings' minds as they got into the car.

And then came the dreaded question that I knew would follow their arrival: "Can we please have a snack?"

Now at this point, I could pretend that in between starting and restarting the washer this morning I had planned ahead and made some cute little ants-on-a-log and some vanilla wafers with all-natural peanut butter nestled between them. But who am I trying to kid here? My frazzled mind was racing at this point, trying to justify whether to spend too much on a spur-of-the-moment snack out or go home and throw some plastic-wrapped delicacy at my kiddos. I was also deciding if I really wanted to part with the last five dollars I had.

I opted for another thing: I took them to the Dollar Store and let them spend a dollar each on some handheld ice cream treat of their choice. I could see them as they raced in, dollar in hand, peering with the most curious of eyes into the freezer, searching for something irresistible.

For one, it was the chocolate, nut-covered ice cream bar. For the other, the same but with strawberry.

And then I saw something else I rarely take the time to witness: sheer, childish delight.

I tried to resist the constant urge to remind them to lick the edges and not let it drip everywhere. I just let them savor the moment as we drove over to the trash dump to drop off all that trash in the back. And then, realizing it was time to pick up their big brother, we pulled up at the middle school, literally forty-seven minutes before dismissal. (Last time, in my delight to be so early, I had forgotten to turn my car ignition all the way off and you guessed it—dead battery. Right when the bell rang ... right in front of the front doors of the school.)

One child played in the parking lot by the car with a friend (I know, not safe) and the other worked on homework while I pretended to read the novel I had somehow managed to grab on my way out the door sometime earlier in the week.

Here's what I need you to know:
So often, we let our lives get so busy planning things to do and getting to places we think we need to be that we forget these exact moments don't come back. Sometimes, we just need to let them spend the last five dollars. We need to let them get sticky hands and stained faces, and we need to just roll with it.

My little people and your little people—they will never again be in this exact moment. We can spend the minutes we have always being practical and planned, or we can take some time every now and again and just be spontaneous.

Let's try to focus more on embracing the moment—on making memories—before the sun has set on this day. Tomorrow will bring its own set of challenges. Do today. I have never ended a day spent with my little people wishing I had done more chores or seen their faces less.

Follow-up true story: I'm currently sitting in the parking lot of McDonald's, using the free Wi-Fi after dropping the girls off at softball practice and the boy off at baseball. I am drinking nothing because the minions used all my cash today. Remember the little bit I had left after the ice cream? The boy got to enjoy a cold, grape Nehi in a glass bottle and some gummy worms, two of his most favorite splurges ever. And my eldest princess used my debit card last night and forgot to return it to my wallet.

Maybe that makes me poor at the moment, but honestly, I couldn't feel any richer. Being able to just take a few moments and do something out of the ordinary today was a rare blessing for us all, and I intend to let it really sink in … even while I am smelling French fries and feeling rather thirsty.

In other news, I did manage to get dinner cooked before it was time for us to go to practice. Of course, there wasn't time for us to eat it, just time for it to get finished, mostly due to the fact that I spent too much time explaining to my kids that the "burned" top is actually just the barbecue sauce, and the chicken is fine. And also because, for some reason, I always have to read the directions on how to make rice. Even after all these years.

HERE'S WHAT I NEED YOU TO KNOW
{about heat}

The dryer decided to go on strike.

It's been warning me for a little while, showing its disapproval of my load sizes by not heating up and by eating a sock every now and then as a threat before further action. For the most part, it has continued functioning pretty well, but yesterday, when I went to get the clothes that *should* have been warm and ready to be folded, they were still cold and wet.

Instead of rushing straight over to the laundromat to finish the job, I fumbled around, thinking at some point—after I turned all the knobs over and over and opened and closed the door several times—it was going to start working again. I flipped the breaker, consulted the internet, and texted some not-so-nice things in all caps to my husband. None of my techniques helped, which is why I found myself going to the laundromat with two *heaping* loads of wet laundry.

And they weren't two of those "nice" loads that basically have towels and washcloths and the occasional T-shirt or two. No, these loads came about because I threw in yet another single sock/T-shirt/pair of jeans/ pair of underwear and anything else lying around on the floor near the washer and said to myself, "It's going to suck to transfer this to the dryer and fold because there are way too many types of clothes in it."

So it was under these circumstances that I found myself standing there, staring at a rather large commercial-grade dryer as if everything written on it was in a foreign language and I had never done a load of laundry before in my life. When I finally came to my senses, I opened up the door of the dryer and began to load in not one, but both baskets of wet clothes because I was absolutely convinced that the size of the dryer was large enough to do both loads in a timely fashion. (All I will say to this matter is that looks can be deceiving.)

After I finally got everything loaded into the dryer, I closed the door and took a glance at the directions again. It was at this point that I noticed some kind soul had jammed a piece of paper into the coin slot, therefore rendering the dryer totally useless.

Open door.

Unload.

Change dryers.

Reload.

Close the door again.

Stare glassy-eyed at the directions once again.

At some point, I decided that I better come to my senses, or I was going to be standing there all day with wet clothes.

After careful consideration of the instructions, I understood that it took a quarter for some unknown number of minutes. So I turned to the sweet lady standing next to me busily doing her *own* work and asked her how long it usually took her to dry a load. She said, "I usually just start with three quarters."

I decided that was a good place for me to start too.

Quarter in.

Quarter in.

Quarter in.

What did I get for my seventy-five cents?

Twenty-four minutes of peace and quiet.

(I would like to point out that I wish I could purchase twenty-four minutes of peace and quiet at home for a mere seventy-five cents.)

Anyway, I had brought a book, some water, a protein bar, and my phone, so I organized my stuff around me, checked that the dryer was actually working, opened my water bottle, opened the protein bar, located the page I was on in the book (due to the bookmark being missing), and realized, after reading what felt like just a few pages, that twenty-four minutes had passed.

Clearly I had overloaded the dryers; clearly twenty-four minutes was not enough, but I'm not going to lie, when I opened the dryer door to check on the clothes inside, the fact that they were warm—some even hot—was extremely comforting. This felt familiar. This was what my dryer at home was supposed to be doing.

Quarter in.

Quarter in.

Sixteen more minutes to spare … which I then spent looking for loose, escaped clothing in the trunk of my car, emptying the trash that had been collecting piece by piece in my door, organizing the clutter above the visor and, once again, opening my book to devour a few precious pages.

And yep. Sixteen minutes was gone.

Evaporated.

MIA.

By now, the clothes were dry, and I had the task I hate most on this planet: folding.

And let's just say that all those extraneous items I had added, as well as the fact that I hadn't bothered to turn the clothes right side out, made the task even more awful. Folding clothes is the devil's work—I am certain.

But the clothes were warm and smelled nice and felt fresh. So I folded and folded and folded and pondered.

Here's what I need you to know:
My clothes had been tossed around in the washer at home. They had been flipped and turned and twisted and wrung out.

But they were never done, never complete, never finished.

And it occurred to me that the heat made the difference, creating a temperature that caused the water to change forms and disappear—ultimately, drying the clothes.

And God cupped my ear with his faithful hand and whispered to me, "It's the heat that makes the difference. It's my fire and the fire of adversity, combined with my flipping, turning, twisting, and wringing out that makes the work done. Complete. When you find yourself facing impossible odds—that's my heat. When your plans crash around you and you have to start over, I am allowing the flames to spur you into action. Don't ever be afraid of the heat or the flames. I won't let them consume you."

If I am being totally honest, I don't like the heat of life. I don't want to have my world upended by tragedy. I don't want to have to watch my plans not work out like I dreamed. I don't like when there are consequences to my actions.

But I am learning to accept that the heat is the most important part of the process. I am trying harder to lean in and learn the lessons that come with the heat.

Laundry still sucks.

But now when the drying is finished and the folding begins, I am reminded to be thankful for the heat, both in my dryer and in my life, for that is what has made the difference.

HERE'S WHAT I NEED YOU TO KNOW
{about making adjustments}

I have this cabinet that I love. It was given to me many years ago, and it has been well loved by our family. It has held junk food snacks, baking ingredients, and every now and then, healthy foods. Its doors are almost always open. I don't know why no one seems to be able to close them. I am certain I press them closed a minimum of ten times daily.

The cabinet has always had a cute little wobble, and the doors require an extra little push to shut, but it's quaint, it's vintage, and it fits the mood of our home. My decorating style can best be described as: she tried.

Recently, when we had a miniflood that resulted in our kitchen floor having to be replaced, we had to move the cabinet. When the floor was finished, the wall painted, and the trim installed, we moved it back into place.

And it wobbled worse than it ever had.

Like maybe-it's-going-to-topple-over wobbling.

We discussed getting rid of it. After all, it's old, and the doors require a certain amount of tug to open and, according to my family, superhero strength to close. It could, for a cost, be replaced with something new, stylish, and trendy. But ...

I love this cabinet.

So before taking it to the curb, I asked the husband to tilt it sideways and let me see what type of feet it had under it. Much to my excitement, it had adjustable feet. I had no idea. For years it has wobbled, and we have just accepted the fact that it was always going to be that way.

But with a little adjustment, it now is almost like new.

It was uncomfortable to have my fingers under there, twisting those little adjustable feet. It worried me that I might get hurt.

It was frustrating at times having to figure out which way to make the adjustments so that it would sit level.

It was aggravating because I wanted someone to blame for the malfunction. It felt a lot like frustration, work, and wasted effort.

And then, it was right.

It looked right, and it felt right, and it operated as it should.

All because I took the time to make an adjustment rather than start over.

Here's what I need you to know:
Some things start off well for us.

They look right, they feel right, they operate as they should.

And then, they don't.

Sometimes they become that way due to lack of attention. Sometimes there really isn't a reason, and sometimes there's a really huge reason. But for whatever reason, we ponder pulling the plug, calling it quits, starting over.

We are enticed by new, stylish, and trendy.

But often what is wobbly and uncertain is just something that needs a little attention. A little adjustment.

It will feel like frustration.

It will feel like work.

It will feel like wasted effort.

And you might even get hurt.

But the effort pays off in something that will look right, feel right, and operate right.

Making adjustments doesn't mean we will always get it just right along the way.

Don't be talked into giving up because it's hard or frustrating or feels like work. Look for the little wobbles and make some adjustments.

Adjust your friendships.

Adjust your parenting.

Adjust your marriage.

Adjust your schedules and workloads and priorities.

Maybe even adjust your attitude.

This work is what makes things stand tall and steady.

HERE'S WHAT I NEED YOU TO KNOW
{about price tags}

I'm a gift giver. I don't receive gifts well. When someone goes out of their way to give me something, it makes me clammy and uncomfortable and nervous. I am sure it comes across as unappreciative.

The eye contact is awkward. The unexpectedness makes me tense up, and the reaching out to accept the gift turns me into a teenage girl at a middle school dance, complete with sweaty palms and shifty glances.

But *giving* gifts?

That's a totally different story.

I love selecting just the right thing for just the right person. I love finding some treasure while out shopping and knowing exactly who will love it. After that, it's all about the details to me. Packaging that gift up in a way that I know will be loved by the receiver of the gift is where it's at.

I have always believed that love is in the details.

The detail that gets my first attention: taking off the price tag.

Sometimes things cost a lot. Sometimes things are found on sale, and they are less expensive. Sometimes I come across *amazing* things for absolutely free! Regardless, I always start my packaging process with removing the price tag.

Taking off the price tag allows the gift to be seen for its intended value, not its perceived value.

Here's what I need you to know:
It's time for us to take off our price tags.

Stay-at-home mamas, take off your price tags.

Stop letting the world dictate the value of homeschooling and all-day laundry marathons and undivided attention to children. Making meals and rearranging clutter is honorable work. You are the keeper of appointments and the schedule master. Other humans are alive because you make sure life moves forward all day long, every single day.

Know your worth.

Working mamas, take off your price tags.

Stop letting society call you selfish and worldly and uncaring for having a career. Stop allowing others to decide whether your choice of vocation is worth working outside the home for. You might need the outlet or the money, or it might just be that you are truly passionate about the work you are doing.

Know your worth.

Single parents, take off your price tags.

Stop letting your two-parent household friends make you feel unsupported and unworthy and undervalued. Your story is important, and sometimes other people write a chapter or two that maybe we would have left out had we been given the choice. Stop letting your marital status dictate your contribution to society.

Know your worth.

Married friends, take off your price tags.

Stop letting society tell you that staying married is settling or giving up or letting go of your ambitions. Your choice to share your life fully committed to another person is yours to make alone.

Know your worth.

Divorced friends, take off your price tags.

Stop letting people who have not lived in your home decide that you did not work hard enough or do all that could be done. None of us were there in your story. Stop letting people pick up the pen and add to it.

Know your worth.

Childless friends, take off your price tags.

Stop allowing the world to make parenthood the ultimate goal for all couples. Your contributions to this world are not determined by the number of children you either have or do not have. Whether you have consciously chosen to not have children or you have tried and haven't succeeded, stop letting the world decide that offspring are what gives you value.

Know your worth.

Friends of every race and religion and sexual orientation, take off your price tags.

Stop allowing those who have never walked your path tell you how to feel. Every single human has been designed and destined for a purpose, and you are no different. You were created with the master plan in mind. Stop allowing others to make the color of your skin or who you worship or who you love determine if you are worthy or not. If you are breathing, you are loved by the one who designed it all.

Know your worth.

Addicted friends, take off your price tags.

Your struggle is not your destiny. Stop letting your worth be determined by how long you last between pitfalls. Every day that you face your demons is a good day. Stop allowing what *has been* determine what *will be.*

Know your worth.

You are *all* enough.

Take off your price tags, friends.

Your worth is inherent in the price that was paid for you by Christ, and your value is deeply embedded into your very core.

You are worth so much more than you even know.

Know. Your. Worth.

HERE'S WHAT I NEED YOU TO KNOW
{about "watch this"}

Mamas, if you have been at this job long enough for your little people to develop language skills, you are sick and tired of hearing: "Hey, Mom, watch this!"

Don't lie and say you're not.

Don't pretend it doesn't grate your last entire nerve that every single time you remotely focus on anything else, they scream it at the top of their lungs. No matter what the activity, an audience is demanded.

We watch them jump.

We watch them sing.

We watch them put on socks.

We watch them poop, for the love of all things holy.

Every. Single. Time.

Usually, I'm the optimistic type, and I'll pass along some thread of hope to hang onto that this behavior will pass. Usually, I will be the one reminding you to treasure these moments, to add them like snapshots into your long-term memory. That you'll miss "it." That this behavior won't last forever.

But ...

Not this time.

It never ends.

There, I said it.

This behavior will continue up to and beyond twenty-five years of age. That's all I can account for at the current moment. I can, with 100 percent certainty, say that it will continue up until this exact point at the minimum.

Here's what I need you to know:
While the need for us to look and listen will always continue, the pitch of their voices will lower. The intensity with which the words are unleashed will lessen. The language will change, and the verbiage will be more mature.

"Hey, Mom, watch this!" will sound, instead, more like:

"Would you like to see where I work?"

"Let me grab my key so I can stop and check the mail."

"I'm going to start some laundry first."

"I'll pay for lunch."

It will sound like, "I paid my rent on time" or "I bought a house" or "I met someone."

The words are different, but the sentiment is familiar: "Hey, Mom, watch this!"

And I can assure you, hearing it from the adult versions of themselves makes all the times it scrapes against your last bit of sanity totally worth it.

HERE'S WHAT I NEED YOU TO KNOW
{about one day}

We cleaned out and organized the outdoor building.
It's filled with seasonal decorations, luggage, folding chairs, project pieces (that I *will* get to someday), and stuff that has been outgrown and passed on to us. So little of it is my kids' stuff anymore. Most of those things have been donated or thrown away. There are a few mementos, but mostly it's grown-up stuff now.

Lots of old windows for projects.

Several old shutters I have great plans for.

Lots of weathered chairs I plan to sit plants in.

An old box spring that will soon be the most amazing light fixture ever.

Just not a lot of little people's stuff anymore.

It's much the same inside the house these days as well. There are a lot fewer pairs of shoes to trip over (though there are still plenty). There are fewer loads of laundry and fewer chore lists.

We moved two (not so) littles out this summer, and even with three still at home, the air seems quieter. The traffic patterns are less congested. My socks are disappearing less often and my stuff seems to stay put a little more often.

Here's what I need you to know:
In the middle of the crying babies and terrible twos—
When the clock revolves around diaper changes and feedings,
When there is no "me" time,
When date night is a trip to a big box store and filling up the car with gas,
When there's no time to water the plants—or water your soul,
When taking a constantly interrupted bath is frustrating, and you cannot find your keys—again,
But one day, you will miss all that.

One day, you will realize the time change didn't really mess up anyone's schedule.

One day, you won't have to sweep up dirt as often from shoes not taken off at the door.

One day, you won't need a gallon of milk every three days. You won't have to be at three sporting events a week. There won't be papers to sign and tests to study for, and there won't need to be a parental password on your Netflix account anymore to keep the kiddos from stumbling across things you don't want them to see.

And you will miss it all.

The emotion sneaks up and surprises you on days when you think you're just cleaning out the building, and you're reminded that time only moves forward. That is its only direction of travel. **We don't get to redo, not even one single moment.**

So move the shoes that are blocking the walking path, but remember the little people who left them there.

Snuggle those babies a little longer during the middle-of-the-night feedings. Clean up the messes. Wipe the noses. Wonder where all your personal things have gone.

Because one day—soon enough—all the things will be right where you left them.

HERE'S WHAT I NEED YOU TO KNOW
{about tomorrow}

Tomorrow.

Tomorrow is your big day. Tonight, we rehearsed for it.

You walked through the motions and found your place and said your words. This has been much of what raising you has been like.

Rehearsal.

I have walked you through the motions and shown you your place and said the words to you. All the words.

I have taught you all the things I know.

I have tried to hold your heart tenderly while still making sure you understood your responsibilities as an adult.

I have tried to teach you how to make good choices and how to hold your head up high when you haven't done so.

I have tried to teach you how to work hard and be accountable for your actions. Those were very humbling lessons—sometimes for you and sometimes for me.

Here's what I need you to know:

I regret nothing.

I have left it all on the table.

I have put my whole heart into raising you, and I am beyond proud of the person you have become.

I have loved you and hugged you and held you—and now I release you.

There are no words we have left unsaid. There are no chances we have missed. There is no way to quantify our relationship.

I look forward to tomorrow.

I am prouder of you than any words could possibly convey.

Be a good human.

Be gentle.

Be kind.

Be forgiving.

Love fiercely and never, ever quit.

I love you until tomorrow and then again until all the tomorrows have passed.

HERE'S WHAT I NEED YOU TO KNOW
{about normal}

It's 1:44 a.m., and I'm sitting on the porch overlooking the pool on the dreaded last night of vacation.

Beside me is a thirteen-year-old girl I love so very much who is binge-watching a show on Netflix that is supposed to be deleted from the viewing inventory in just a matter of days.

This moment takes me back to rural Georgia many summers past when I took a trip to my grandmother's home. Apparently, we both couldn't sleep, and our paths merged in the dusty living room of her little country house, Grandma in her rocking chair and me on another rickety chair nearby. She was rubbing her knees. They were always sore from years of hard labor in the fields her family worked for a living. Actual hard labor. Actual fields. Real, actual work.

We sat there in silence for a few moments, this rare joining of quiet space between us, the house settling around us. Our thoughts whirled around in the stagnant air briefly before she leaned in close and whispered, "Would you like to share some ice cream?"

My sweet grandmother was poor for as far back as I could remember. She never had extra. She never had luxuries. I didn't expect that she would ever have a treat like ice cream, much less offer it to me in whispered conversation across the stillness of a summer night. That night was a rare glimpse for me into the depths of a woman I had known my entire life, yet maybe never really *knew* until that exact moment. Only a few years after that night, she passed away. I have so many memories, but the one I hold dearest is of a summer night when we both couldn't sleep and met at the living room chairs.

Here's what I need you to know:
Sometimes what's usual and normal needs to be shaken up a bit.

Sometimes we need the silence.

Sometimes we need the conversation.

Sometimes we need the ice cream.

I'm not an advocate of late-night binge-watching TV for adolescents normally, but I will forever be an advocate of middle-of-the-night stolen moments when the air is stiff with expectation.

The days are short, and they are numbered. I have no idea how many this child of mine and I will get, so for tonight, we will sit side by side, and I will inhale the beauty of the moment. **For in these moments, I am refreshed, refilled, and reminded that I only have her here on God's schedule.**

The gems are hidden deep, my friends. We have to dig for them most often. But occasionally, we stumble across one on the surface of our lives, and in those moments, we must remember to grab hold and make the most of what we have been blessed with.

HERE'S WHAT I NEED YOU TO KNOW
{about bricks}

A while back, we went to say our final goodbyes to Mema and Papa's house.

I need it to be understood right here and now: I had the best in-laws humanly possible. Mema was my mother-in-awe, if you will. She was the keeper of the shoe sizes and the teller of stories and the master coloring-book filler. She knew the kids' ever-changing favorite characters and their favorite places to eat. She would search high and low for things they loved and places they would love to go. Sometimes her visits would be less than twenty-four hours long, yet when she left, the vacuum of energy and excitement was palpable.

Papa was the teacher. He was forever showing the kids about tractors and gun safety and how to make the world's "Second Best Baked Bean" recipe. He laughed at their ridiculous antics and tolerated more than his fair share of nonsense. He never raised his voice. His demeanor brought even the worst behavior into check. He taught them love through lessons.

Our lives are somehow less without them here. They embraced grandparenthood like one holds onto a valuable treasure: tightening and readjusting as needed so as to always maintain a firm grip.

Losing a loved one is continuous. You don't lose someone once; you are constantly in a state of loss. Every time I remember something I want to tell them, I lose them again. When the kids have a big event,

I am reminded that I cannot share that with them. When our people start moving out of our home and making their own homes elsewhere, I know these will be places my in-laws will never see or visit, and the loss of that moment is painful. When wedding invitations need to be addressed and parties are planned, the thought is always there: they would have loved every second of this.

Sometimes it is the loss of future moments that hurt almost worse than the loss of the now.

At that final goodbye, there was so much to pack up and deal with. Mema was an equal-opportunity collector. She collected flower-arranging materials and loose buttons and Christmas sweatshirts. She was always adding a new "pretty" to her collection of ceramic knickknacks. She saved old magazines, lighthouse décor, and plastic containers in equal measure. Nothing went to waste.

Papa was the same with his tools. If it was available, he had three. If you needed a hammer or a chainsaw or a roll of black electrical tape, he was your guy. And he never made you feel silly for asking. He took delight in finding just what was needed for every situation. He did that with our hearts as well.

Holding items that held so much meaning to others is hard. We all find different values in the same item. And everything seems to tell a story. When you can't keep everything, it's hard to decide what holds the most value. When you know how much someone else loved something, it's even harder to loosen the grip.

We sorted and we organized and we agonized.

We kept things we loved, and we kept some things just because we knew they loved them.

Weeks after the packing of the boxes and the final shutting of the door, I found an old brick on the floor inside the front door of our home. It seemed oddly out of place, but when so many people live in such a small space, one learns not to ask too many questions.

Some time passed, and I realized the brick was still there. I usually let things alone for a bit, being eternally optimistic that whoever left the thing there will actually come back to get it.

I am usually wrong. Normally, I end up picking the thing up and taking it wherever it belongs.

The brick was no different, but I didn't actually know where it belonged. I love old farmhouse-looking decor (yet do not live on a farm or in an actual farmhouse), so I decided to put the brick on the Hoosier cabinet that was brought home from my in-laws' house at the request of my husband.

The brick sat there for a while without anyone seeming to notice. Then one day after football practice, my middle came in and without missing a beat pronounced: "I see you found my brick. Thanks. That came from Mema and Papa's house, and I wanted to keep it in memory of them."

I was dumbfounded. I remembered while we had been cleaning things out, he had been outside walking around. I figured he was a typical seventeen-year-old boy and had no interest in sorting through stuff that meant so little to him. Or that maybe he was just too emotional to help. Either way, I let him be.

I realize now that while we were all *inside* sorting through the things we thought held the value, he was *outside* finding the real gem.

This seemingly useless item—this lone, old brick—held memories for him. It was a symbol of the times they had spent hanging out on the family land, learning the lessons that would last forever. **Life isn't about what we have or who we know; it's about who we are and what we build.**

Our memories. Our legacy.

Here's what I need you to know:
Give your things away while you're alive. Tell the stories that go with the things. Let your people take them home to enjoy while you're still alive to see it and hear about it. Chances are, after you're gone, it won't be the stuff they want anyway. It'll be the memories and the stories—the things that shape their lives and give them a firm foundation.

It'll be the bricks.

They will want the bricks.

HERE'S WHAT I NEED YOU TO KNOW
{about showing up}

I think if I've learned anything from my life so far, it's this: just show up.

Just show up for your kids.

Just show up for your friends.

Just show up for your coworkers.

Just show up in your less-than Sunday best.

Just show up—even if you're late.

Just show up—burdened or lonely or in need.

Just show up for yourself. *Please*, show up for yourself. Be your own best friend, your closest confidant, your biggest advocate. If you have to show up angry, just show up.

If you have to show up hurting, just show up.

If the only way you can show up is lost or bitter or robbed of all hope, just please show up.

If you're stuck at a dead end, show up lost.

If you've tried over and over and over again, show up weary.

If you're certain you can't take another breath or another step or another hurt, show up desperate.

Just please show up.

Here's what I need you to know:
If you're living your best life, show up eager.

If you have all you need, show up generously.

If you've been forgiven, show up with mercy.

If you've survived, show up with your story.

Just show up.

Show up for the weak.

Show up for the strong.

Show up when it's easy, and show up when it's the last thing you feel like doing.

Just show up.

We all have our off days. All of us. But we can't help each other if we don't all show up. **Today, you might need me. Tomorrow, I might need you.**

Please, just show up.

HERE'S WHAT I NEED YOU TO KNOW
{about motherhood}

I see you.

I see you at the park, walking the track, trying to wish the muffin-top calories away while the younger moms push littles on the swings and play chase. I recognize the relief that you are not needed to play such a pivotal role at the park, and yet at the same time I see the misty-eyed way you watch and remember those days.

I see you at the water park and the pool, trying to keep an eye on your oh-so-independent kids while trying to negotiate whether to sit closest to the gorgeous young moms in bikinis or the pregnant moms who look more similar to your current body shape. I sense you trying to decide if the swimsuit you finally selected is current enough to make your middle school kids not want to walk ten feet apart from you.

I get it; I really do.

I see you grocery shopping more slowly, trying to remember who will be at dinner that night since some work, and some are away with friends, and some just don't want to join you at the table for meals anymore.

I hear the insecurity in your voice as you try to have meaningful conversations with your nearing-adulthood children. I recognize the quiet way you ask how things are going because you don't want to be thought of as prying ... and yet not asking is risking that they will think you don't care.

Every part of motherhood feels risky.

I see you at the pharmacy, refilling your prescription for the hormones that will hopefully keep you from snapping like a dead twig (and ending with a mug shot that shows up when your kids look up your name on the internet years from now).

I see you on vacation by the pool alone because all your people are tired or bored or so engulfed in technology that you can't pry them out of the hotel or condo or house.

I see you all over.

When do I see you the most?

I see you every time I look in the mirror and notice a new crease or wrinkle or "beauty mark."

I see you because I *am you too.*

I am right there, like you, looking back and wondering where time went while looking ahead and wondering how much time is left. I am with you at the park and the pool, the grocery store and the pharmacy.

I am asking the same questions in the same timid voice to the same almost-adults, hoping for the same connection.

And you are me. We feel like we have lost so much time, and we wonder if we've done enough or held on enough or let go enough. Have we *been* enough?

But oh my friends, look what we have gained.

Here's what I need you to know:

We get to have dinner out without high chairs or kids' menus.

We don't have to grab a stroller and struggle with its setup and its takedown to go each and every place.

We get to do girls' weekends without worrying if someone is using too much breast milk while feeding our baby back at home. We can read more and travel more and think more. We get to discover a new person buried deep inside the cloak of "mom" and looking in the rearview mirror we call experience, we get to decide who she is and how she acts and what she does. We get to have spontaneous pedicures and lunch out alone, and we get to browse the aisles of the library that are actually made for adults. We get to forget anything and everything, our clothes don't necessarily have to be in style, we get to laugh at our own jokes and cry at sappy movies, and we get to blame it all on being older.

We don't even have to care what anybody else thinks.

We get to look back on these people we have given our hearts and souls for, some of us even our careers for, and we get to watch them grow and thrive and become amazing adults.

We did that.

We need each other, friend.

Right around the corner or in the next cubicle or even sitting in the next row on Sunday is someone just like you. Someone who has just wrapped up years of clipping Box Tops for Education, packing mediocre lunches, and attending sports events, performances, and awards ceremonies.

Right near you is someone who could use a lunch date or a day trip to the beach or just a meaningful conversation about life.

Someone just like you.

And someone just like me.

HERE'S WHAT I NEED YOU TO KNOW
{about mothers-in-law}

There are a few things I have wanted to say to you for a long time. Some of them are long overdue, but I have heard there is no better time than the present, so I am just going to lay this all out there.

I knew from the moment we met that we were totally different types of people. I knew that I would *never* be like you in many ways. I knew from the moment I saw you come upstairs from the basement—where you were hard at work doing laundry—to refill your husband's tea glass that I was never going to be like that. Seriously. You walked across the length of the house and up two sets of stairs to refill a man's tea glass. A man who, I might add, was literally sitting at the table ... in the kitchen. No ma'am, that is not how I am wired.

I had no idea when we first met that day I would be your daughter-in-law. I didn't know that our lives would forever be intertwined by a web of relatives and events and phone calls and family gatherings.

I had no idea that bringing my kids to see you would always involve such chaos. It's clear that my desire for organization and your desire to just be "in the moment" didn't mesh at times. I cannot count the number of times I had to remind my kids to get dressed and clean themselves up before bounding out to see you for breakfast. I didn't think it was illogical to expect them to do that. Clearly, our brains functioned differently. Countless times you called me to ask the kids birthdates … and their ages … and their sizes … and their favorite music/toys/ games/shows. You were always calling to update the list of their current wants and needs.

Here's what I need you to know:
I don't think like you.

I don't act like you.

I don't dress like you or cook like you or even like the same type of music as you. I don't raise my kids the same way you did. I haven't learned to just leave the dishes until a better time or ever felt the need to pack five or six bags for an overnight stay. Every time you came to our house it looked like a Samsonite luggage display at Kohl's.

And don't get me started on what a shopping trip with you was like. I seriously cannot even grasp why every trip to any store turned into a daylong journey. It had nothing to do with your health or your ability to get around. It did have everything, however, to do with your desire to look at literally each and every item a store had for sale. It didn't matter if it was Walmart or Belk or the gift section of a gas station. It all had to be seen. And we all had to loiter around and wait for you to be done looking.

We are so different.

But here's the thing: Last November, I lost you.

I say *lost* because that is how I have felt since you were taken away so suddenly on a normal Thursday a week before Thanksgiving.

I have a head full of stories to share and a phone full of pictures and a carload of kids, and you are gone. Just gone.

And all of a sudden I realize all that you taught me.

It never mattered to you if I ever refilled your son's glass of tea or not. You loved me anyway. If I wanted the kids to get dressed and clean up before breakfast, you were right there, encouraging them to obey and smiling all the while.

Yes, you called me often for the kids' sizes. Often. But that's also because you bought all their Easter clothes and school clothes. You filled massive Easter baskets and put Santa to shame when it came to

Christmas. Birthdays were enormous events, and you never hesitated to make the two-plus-hour trip to celebrate a birthday or graduation or holiday or just to have lunch.

And I am at a total loss as to how I will ever fill those shoes.

We fumbled through Thanksgiving and Christmas in a fog. Easter came, and it felt so physically painful to ponder what to dress the kids in. And now it's almost time for back-to-school shopping, and I have no idea how to do it. You made it special and fun and memorable, and those moments are etched indelibly on my heart.

I cannot be you.

I have been blessed with a mother … a wonderful mother. And she is here. She is present, and she loves my kids. But she is not you.

She fills a spot that is hers to fill, and your spot feels like a gaping wound—a void that I will never be able to fill.

Thank you for always telling me you loved me and that I was needed and wanted and appreciated. Thank you for holding me when I failed. Thank you for lifting my heart when it was broken. Thank you for staring me in the face and reminding me that I have worth and value and that my contributions to the world are only mine to make. Thank you for helping me live with no regrets.

Thank you from the bottom of my heart for being the physical embodiment of unconditional love.

Your presence is so missed. My heart feels the loss with such great magnitude. We all struggle with looking forward to big events, knowing you won't be there to laugh and cry and celebrate with us. I am so grateful that we loved big, and we shared our hearts with each other. Thank you for being vulnerable with me and for never hiding behind your story. Thank you for being you.

There will never be another you. I recognize that.

This void will, in some way, always be here as a reminder.

Things that leave big holes are things that filled big spaces.

You filled my space with love, and I am forever grateful.

Your daughter-in-love forever,

Shari

HERE'S WHAT I NEED YOU TO KNOW
{about endings}

I was watching a movie recently that came highly recommended. It was one of those movies that everyone was talking about. Highly anticipated. Full of A-list actors. Produced with a sizeable budget and surrounded by lots of fanfare.

So, I did as I seldom take the time to do, and I popped some popcorn and settled under a fluffy blanket to enjoy this cinematic treasure. I silenced the phone and prayed for no interruptions.

The movie was amazing, just as I had been told. The plot was rich with highs and lows. The characters were intriguing and left me wanting to be friends with them all. The conversations were believable, and I watched the movie almost on the edge of my seat ... until the ending.

I cannot make sense of movies with poor endings. How does a team of people trained to know what the audience wants to see and hear get it so wrong? How could they have possibly thought that was the outcome anyone saw coming or wanted?

I was beyond disappointed. If I had had my way, I am sure I could have brought the entire thing to a more palatable conclusion. But no one asked me, and so I sat there, blankly staring at the screen long after the credits had finished scrolling by.

And then it hit me: the ending may not have been the one I foresaw or wanted, but it still made for a beautiful story.

Here's what I need you to know:
Every one of us has a story to tell. We have a script we have been writing since our birth, and it is ours and ours alone.

Like a book, many of us have chapters we are not proud of. We have parts we wish we could leave out or have unremembered.

But do you know what part people remember most?

The ending.

They won't remember most of the things you hid your head in shame about. They won't recall the words you fumbled over or the dumb choices you made in your uninformed years. They won't be able to retell your parenting fails or the moments you nearly crumbled under the pressure.

They will remember how you finished.

The story isn't over until you take your last breath.

Every day is a new chance.

Twist the plot.

Deepen the relationships.

Start a new chapter.

Change the ending.

You are the author of the most beautiful story you could ever tell: yours.

If you aren't happy with the story so far, turn the page and start fresh. You don't even have to wait until the ink is dry on the last chapter to start again.

Write yourself a beautiful ending.

Acknowledgments

Writing this book seemed easy compared with finding adequate words to express my gratefulness to the masses of people who have supported me and helped make this work happen. I know, even as I begin to formulate a list of specific people, that I will miss some, if not many. So, I will start with a huge "thank you" to every person who has prayed for, given to, and, in unlimited ways, supported this dream of mine. Your acts of kindness and selfless support never went unnoticed. I am forever grateful.

To my husband, Shannon: Thank you for always reminding me I am not too old to dream or chase my dreams and for allowing the simple words "I need to write" to give me a pass to walk away from some obligations so I could write down everything that was swirling around in my head. I love you, and I am beyond grateful for your support.

To Taylor, Logan, Isaac, Rileigh, and Raegan, the ones who call me "Momma": So many of the stories written on these pages came from my moments with you. I am the person I am because of each of you. There is no way to truly convey how proud I am of you all. Watching you grow has been my greatest gift. Thank you for your unlimited forgiveness, unwavering support, and endless jokes. Thank you for never making me initiate the calls and for always opening your lives and your homes to me. I love you all beyond words.

To my mother, Judy: You taught me to love books from an early age. One of my fondest memories was a day when I was home from school and was forbidden to watch television since I was "sick." Instead, I read five *Nancy Drew* books, and I was hooked on words forever. Thanks for always asking, "Have you read this yet?" And for always being willing to lend me your latest purchases to read. I guess I owe you a free copy.

To my siblings, Michelle, Allen, and Robin: Thank you for always allowing me to show up on your doorsteps, overstay my welcome, and talk too much about my kids. I liked growing up with you all, but I love knowing you as adults. You each have a keen sense of humor, and you never cease to make me wish we had just a little bit longer for each visit. I love you all, and I am proud to be your sister.

To my lifelong best friend, Anna Reeves: There simply are no words. You are the keeper of all my secrets. You share my thoughts with a single glance. You never meet a stranger, and you literally know someone every place we travel to. You are the bravest person I know, and I am better for knowing you. Thank you for always reminding me I am a survivor, and don't forget the RV we are buying to travel in when we are old. The world is not ready for what we have planned.

To the Warren Publishing team, Mindy Kuhn, Amy Ashby, Melissa Long, and Erika Nein: I clicked "Submit" filled with hopes, dreams, and ridiculously grandiose plans. You all have made each of those hopes and dreams come true. You have done so much more than correct my grammar, redirect my focus, and make this book a reality. You have allowed me to believe in myself, and you have provided a well-established map for me to follow for this process as well as provided constant encouragement. Thank you all for not making my work feel small and for helping my thoughts find a voice on the pages.

To one of the best teachers and humans I know, Casey Layman: Thank you for always allowing me to get therapy on your couch and for always reminding me of my worth. I was wrong all those years ago when we met, and I thought you couldn't add to my life. Your contributions are never ending, and I am so grateful I can practice being a grandmother with Easton. You are such a great human, and I am so glad my sweet girl landed in your first-grade class all those years ago.

To my friend, Amy Gonzalez: You may have been the very first person to tell me to write a book. Regardless, you are the reason I found the amazing team of women who are making this dream a reality. Thank you for your fierce hugs and your life-giving encouragement. I am sure you had no idea so long ago when our paths crossed that you would play such a pivotal role in making this book find its covers. Thank you.

To my life-giving group chat girls, Holly Ruppe, Lara Hull, and Shannon Estes: I love how most of our conversations begin with a meme and zero context, and we just say what is on our minds. Thank you all for encouraging me to trust the process and for always reminding me this would all be worth it. I love you all, and I am grateful for your transparent friendship. You are rare gems.

To my twice-a-year boss, Kim Willaby: Too many years ago to count, when I was drowning in a sea of worthlessness, you offered me a job. I don't know if we had ever even had a conversation up to that point. You told me you thought I would be a good fit, and that was that. Thank you for helping me get my head above the surface of the waves. Your friendship is a life raft, and your authenticity is the paddle I steer with. I don't say it enough, but I am forever grateful.

To my get-in-there-early-and-get-it-done workout buddies, Megan Joye, Kristi Gragg, and Jacquie Fanning: The number of times our workouts have talked me off a ledge is innumerable. Thank you for being some of the realest people I know. Thanks for always pushing me to be my best self and for not letting me quit, even when I am dissatisfied with each and every song that plays, and I complain the entire time. You have given me strength, both literally and figuratively. Spartan Race, anyone?

To two of my favorite authors on the planet whom I am also blessed to call my friends, Jennifer Niven and Angelo Surmelis: Thank you for being brave with your words and for paving the way for others to write their truths unashamedly. Your work is astounding, and I am so grateful for your friendships.

Last, but certainly not least, thank you God for giving me the ability to write so the words make sense. I know every good gift comes from You, and I am thankful every day for Your grace and mercy. I am nothing without You, and these words are nothing without Your inspiration.

CPSIA information can be obtained
at www.ICGtesting.com
Printed in the USA
BVHW041331290422
635584BV00002B/44